NATIONAL GEOGRAPHIC

Map Essentials

**A Comprehensive Map Skills Program
from National Geographic
School Publishing**

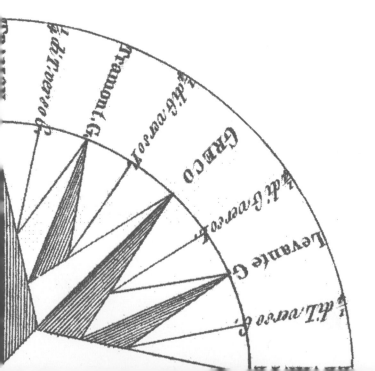

© 2001 National Geographic Society, Washington, D.C. 20036
All rights reserved.

⊛ Printed on recycled paper.

Product #29064
ISBN 0-7922-9025-9

Contents

Searching the Global Grid

Key Ideas

Each degree of latitude and of longitude is made up of 60 **minutes**.

1°

60'

"Houston, we've got a problem." With these chilling words, Jim Lovell, commander of the 1970 Apollo 13 moon mission, reported that an explosion had rocked the spacecraft. If the crew were able to return to Earth at all, where would they come down? Government scientists studied computer information and global grids. A **global grid** is the pattern on a world map formed by intersecting lines of latitude and longitude. They determined that the spacecraft would land at or near specific coordinates in the South Pacific Ocean. **Coordinates** are a set of latitude and longitude measurements that define a point on the global grid. There, over 140 hours after liftoff, the United States Navy plucked the grateful crew from the water.

Coordinates can be very precise. Degrees are broken into small units called **minutes**. Sixty minutes equal one degree. The symbol for minutes is '.

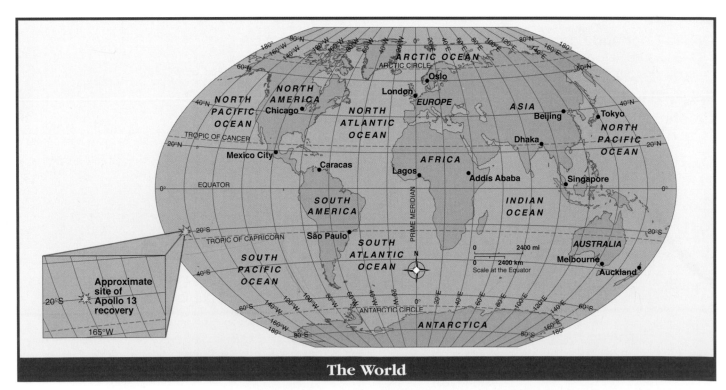

The World

- Look at the map on the previous page. The world map has a grid at intervals of 20°. To find other points you need to estimate. For example, find the city of Oslo, Norway. It is located on a line of latitude, 60° N, which is labeled on the map. It is located about halfway between longitude lines 0° and 20° E. Its coordinates can be estimated as 60° N, 10° E.

- Find the approximate site of the Apollo 13 recovery. What are the coordinates?

- Find the Tropic of Cancer. It lies at 23° 30' N (say 23 degrees, 30 minutes) latitude. That means it is halfway between 23° N and 24° N.

On Your Own

1. Find the Tropic of Capricorn. Estimate its latitude.

2. Find the Arctic Circle. Estimate its latitude. Do the same for the Antarctic Circle.

3. Which city shown on the map is located very close to the Equator? Estimate its coordinates.

Think Like a Geographer

4. How was the global grid a helpful tool for the successful recovery of the Apollo 13 spacecraft and crew?

5. Explain how using minutes makes it possible to measure latitude and longitude more precisely.

Map Fact

State Your Location, Please

Today, the Global Positioning System (GPS) makes it possible to calculate the latitude and longitude of a location more easily than ever. Because of 24 satellites circling the globe, anyone with a handheld GPS receiver can tell exactly where he or she is—to within a few feet. GPS receivers installed in cars give drivers their exact locations and can help drivers plot where they want to go.

Consider This! Why might a GPS receiver be valuable to a land surveyor? A climber nearing the summit of Mount Everest? A sailboat captain?

See NATIONAL GEOGRAPHIC magazine, "Revolutions in Mapping," February 1998, pages 6–39 (pages 31–32 refer to GPS).

Recovery of the Apollo 13 spacecraft and crew

2 Using Map Projections

Cartographers have developed a variety of map **projections** to show spherical Earth on a flat map.

How can something that is flat show something that is a sphere, with complete accuracy? That question has perplexed cartographers for centuries. The answer is that flat maps cannot show every part of Earth with complete accuracy. There is always some kind of **distortion**—a shift in the size or shape of the continents, in distance, or in direction. According to geographer Mark Monmonier, "Even a good map tells a multitude of little white lies."

In an effort to minimize distortion and represent Earth as accurately as possible, cartographers have developed different techniques. Because they transfer, or "project," information from a globe to a flat surface, these methods are called **projections**. Each map projection has advantages and disadvantages.

During the Age of Exploration of the 1400s and 1500s, ship navigators had to plot longer and longer courses. They needed maps that showed accurate shapes of landmasses and true directions from one place to another.

In 1569, the Dutch cartographer Gerardus Mercator (Latin for his real name, Gerhard Kremer) developed the projection later named after him—the **Mercator projection**. This is an early map that uses this projection.

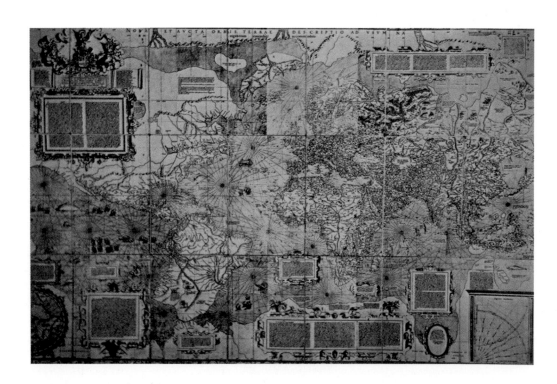

Mercator Projection

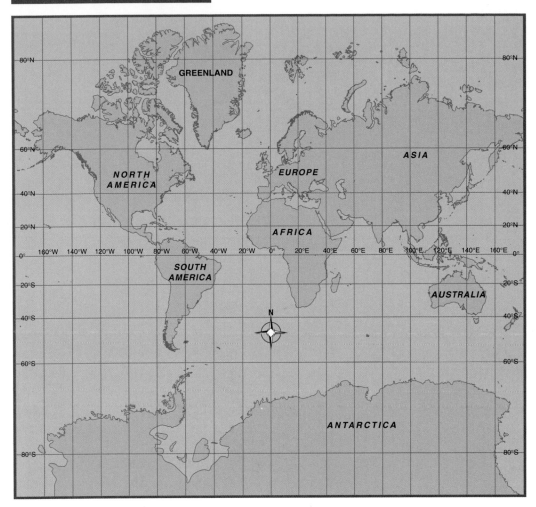

- Note that lines of longitude on the Mercator projection do not meet at the North and South Poles, as they do on a globe. This results in distortion of size in the northern and southern parts of the map.

- Find Greenland on the Mercator projection. Now compare it to Greenland on a globe. The Mercator projection makes Greenland appear much larger than it really is. Areas near the Equator are less distorted than land areas near the poles.

Goode's Projection

- **Goode's projection** is a short way of referring to Goode's Interrupted Homolographic Modified projection. This projection "interrupts" the map near the Poles in order to correct size distortions. It almost looks as though the cartographer has cut a globe apart and laid it flat on paper.

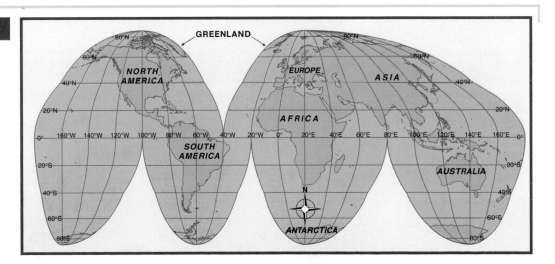

- Find the lines of longitude on Goode's projection. Note that they come closer together at the poles than on the Mercator.

- Find Greenland on Goode's projection and compare it to Greenland on the Mercator projection. What differences do you see?

Winkel Tripel Projection

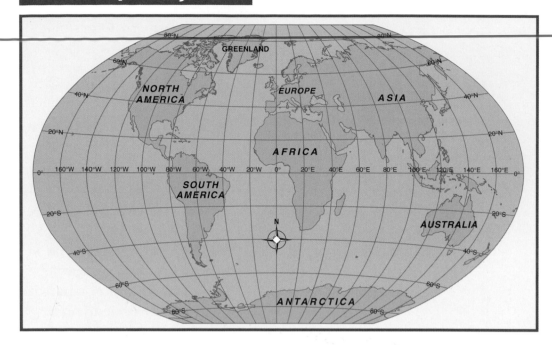

- The **Winkel Tripel projection** is a newer projection now used by the National Geographic Society. Like Goode's projection, it is an equal-area projection. This means it shows all regions of Earth in their correct relative size.

- Find the lines of longitude on the Winkel Tripel projection. Then compare lines of longitude on all three projections. Which have lines that are similar?

- Find Greenland on the Winkel Tripel projection. Now compare it to the other two projections, as well as the satellite image on this page. Which map projection shows Greenland with the least distortion?

- Try comparing other landmasses that are visible in the satellite image to the way they appear in the three map projections.

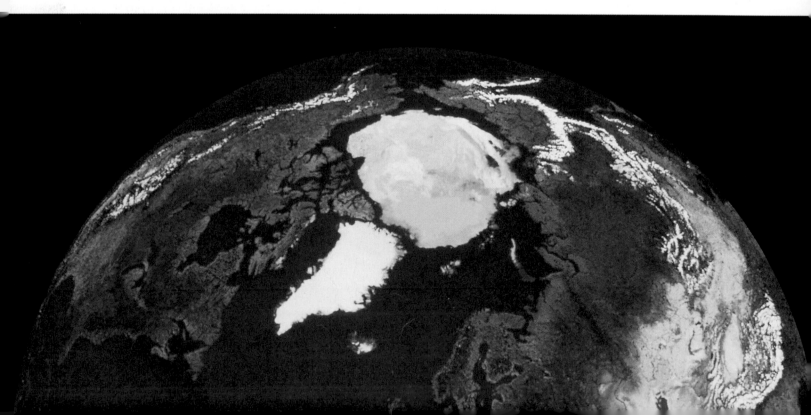

Use the information on pages 6, 7, and 8 to answer the questions below.

1. Where is most of the landmass distortion on a Mercator projection?

2. How are the lines of longitude on the Mercator projection different from those on the other two projections?

3. How does a cartographer lessen distortions in size and shape by curving lines of longitude?

4. How has the Goode's projection been "interrupted"?

5. How does this "interruption" make a flat map more like a globe?

6. Which of the three projections are equal-area projections?

7. Which of the three projections distorts the polar areas the least?

Think Like a Geographer

8. Why do flat map projections create distortions?

9. Why do Goode's and the Winkel Tripel projections create less distortion than the Mercator projection?

NATIONAL GEOGRAPHIC

Map Fact

Mapping in Ancient Times

"Maps, like faces, are the signature of history," wrote American historian Will Durant. And people started making maps thousands of years ago. One of the earliest "map projections" that has come down through time was carved into a flat stone in 600 B.C., pictured at the right. Made by Babylonians, who lived in the ancient Middle East, the map shows Babylonia in the center. Through it runs a line that stands for the Euphrates River, and around Babylonia are circles representing neighboring kingdoms. An ocean surrounds them all.

Consider This! Compare the Babylonians' view of the world to what we know now. How has our knowledge of the world changed?

See NATIONAL GEOGRAPHIC magazine, "Revolutions in Mapping," February 1998, pages 6–39.

3 Physical Regions and the Changing Earth

Key Ideas

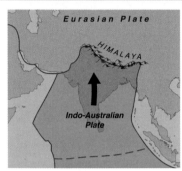

Physical regions, such as the Himalaya, in Asia, have been created by movements of Earth's **tectonic plates**.

"The Roof of the World." "The Third Pole." Those are just two of the names given to Earth's highest mountain range, the mighty Himalaya of South Asia. Centuries ago, when people first started climbing these rocky peaks, they saw outlines of sea creatures in the rock—the fossilized remains of fish and sea shells. The ocean was hundreds of miles away. How could there have been fish at these high elevations?

About a hundred years ago, Physical geographers began to find the answer. They thought that Earth's outer shell resembles a cracked eggshell. Earth's shell is cracked into many rigid pieces they named **tectonic plates**. Some are large; for example, one plate lies beneath most of the Pacific Ocean. Others are smaller, but often still large enough to include an entire continent. These plates move—sometimes scraping past and sometimes colliding into one another—at the rate of up to four inches a year. Earth scientists call this movement **continental drift**.

The Himalaya Range in Tibet

Continental Drift

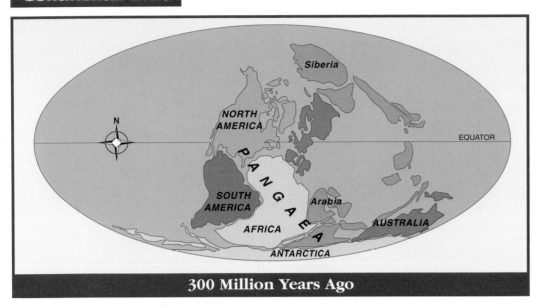

300 Million Years Ago

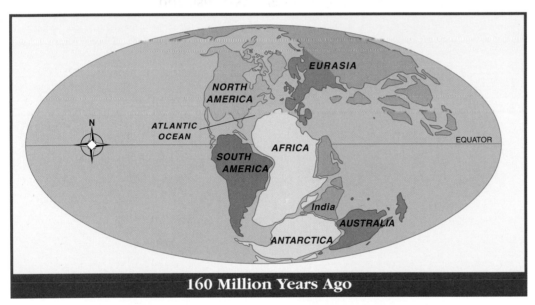

160 Million Years Ago

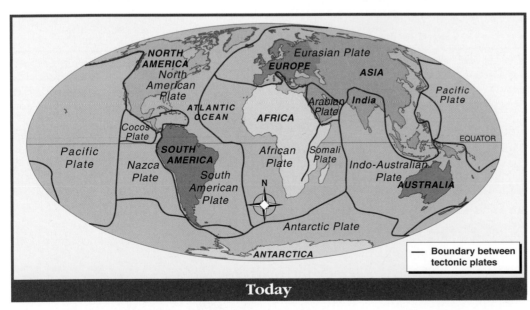

— Boundary between tectonic plates

Today

- The first map shows the tectonic plates about 300 million years ago. The continents were massed into one large "supercontinent" that scientists have named **Pangaea**.

- Find North America on the map of Pangaea. What line of latitude was at its center? Look at the third map to see if this line passes through North America today.

- The second map shows the breakup of Pangaea about 160 million years ago. Find the landmass labeled India on the second map. In what direction was it drifting?

- The third map shows the major tectonic plates today. You can see that India has moved considerably and now abuts the Eurasian plate.

Physical Regions

Millions of years ago, India was a landmass of its own, far from the rest of Asia. Its path put it on a collision course with the Eurasian plate—and what a collision it was! As the Indo-Australian plate struck the Eurasian plate, it ground beneath the Eurasian plate, pushing up land that had once been underwater or at sea level. As the Indo-Australian plate continued its relentless push, the land rose, forming the towering Himalaya mountains. Land that was once under the ocean now towers nearly six miles above sea level! That is why fossilized remains of sea animals can be found at the Himalaya's high elevations.

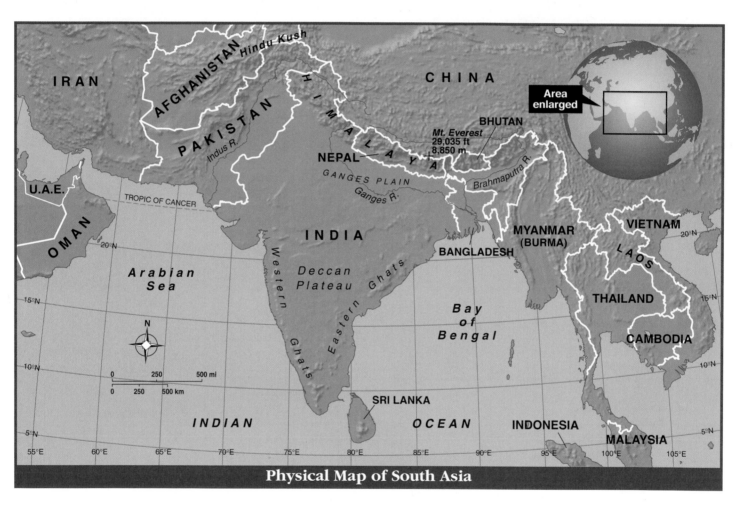

Physical Map of South Asia

- This map shows physical regions of South Asia. A **physical region** is a region that shares certain common features, such as mountains or plains. The Himalaya is a physical region. Find the Himalaya on the map.

- This map also shows **relief**, a map technique that uses shading to show differences in elevation. What can you tell about the relief of the Indian subcontinent? What physical regions do you see?

- Find the Ganges Plain. This fairly low-lying and flat physical region is named after the major river that runs through it. Locate the Ganges River. Lands along large rivers are often plains regions.

Use the information on pages 11 and 12 to help answer the questions.

1. In Pangaea, where was Africa in relation to South America?

2. Where was India in relation to Australia?

3. Which of the seven continents seems to have drifted the least over 300 million years?

4. What tectonic plate borders much of the western part of the North American plate today?

5. What tectonic plate borders much of the western part of the South American plate today?

6. What physical region spreads across much of the interior of India?

7. What technique is often used to show physical differences in elevation on maps?

8. How are the Himalaya and the Hindu Kush similar physical features?

Think Like a Geographer

9. How do the mountains of the Himalaya show evidence of continental drift?

10. Which physical region would you expect to be more heavily populated, the Ganges Plain or the Himalaya? Why?

NATIONAL GEOGRAPHIC
Map Fact

A New Sea?

Unlike major tectonic plates, such as the gigantic Pacific plate, some plates are quite small, such as the Somali plate in East Africa. It is pulling away from the African plate, just as Arabia did millions of years ago. If this movement continues, in about 30 million years water will pour into the East African Rift System from the Indian Ocean and form a new sea.

Consider This! Look at the Atlas map of the world on pages 68–69. What sea was formed when tectonic movement pulled Arabia away from Africa?

See NATIONAL GEOGRAPHIC magazine, "Africa's Great Rift," May 1990, pages 2-41.

These ridges and valleys in Eritrea, Africa, are part of the East African Rift System.

Elevation and Contour Maps

Cartographers show elevation with elevation maps and **contour maps**.

You are planning a trip to Acadia National Park. This park is located on Mount Desert Island in Maine. If you decide to go hiking or biking, what kind of terrain can you expect? Will you be covering fairly flat land with ease or will climbing it leave you huffing and puffing?

As the photograph below of Mount Desert Island shows, the land surface of Earth is highly uneven. Low-lying areas can dip even lower than sea level, while mountainous areas can rise many thousands of feet. Cartographers use different kinds of maps to show elevation. You studied one such map, a relief map, in the last activity.

Acadia National Park on Mount Desert Island, Maine

Using an Elevation Map

An elevation map uses different colors to signal differences in an area's elevation above sea level. Each color represents a different range of elevation. For example, in the elevation map below, dark green shows land from sea level to 300 feet and medium green shows land from 300 feet to 600 feet. The map key matches the colors to their elevation ranges.

The line of profile below the map shows elevation in a different way. A **profile** is a view of something from the side. If you cut Mount Desert along the profile line shown on the map, as you might cut a slice of cake, you would see its elevations from the side.

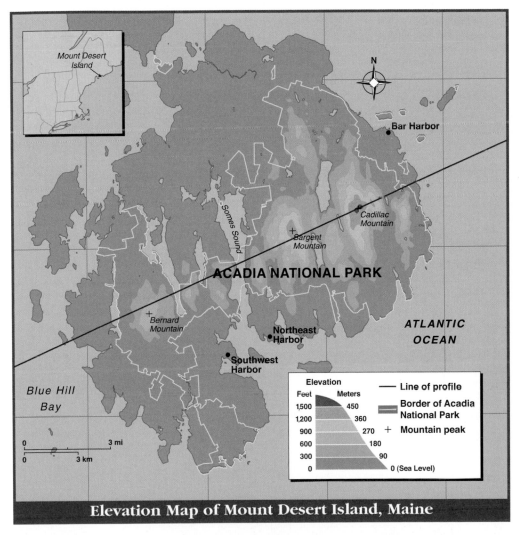

Elevation Map of Mount Desert Island, Maine

- Find the northwestern part of Mount Desert Island. Would hiking or biking here be easy or difficult? Why?

- If you wanted to hike in the highest elevations of Acadia National Park, where on the island would you go?

- Look at the line of profile. Notice that Cadillac Mountain is taller than Sargent Mountain. Both are taller than Bernard Mountain. You can see this "at a glance" by looking at the profile line. To get this information from the map, you would need to study the map and then refer to the key.

- Most of Mount Desert Island falls in which elevation range? Did you use the line of profile or elevation map? Why?

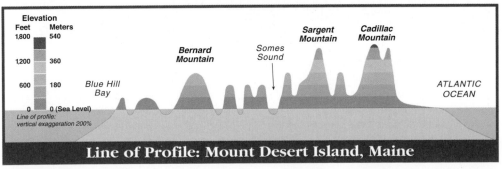

Line of Profile: Mount Desert Island, Maine

15

Using a Contour Map

Another way to show elevation is with a **contour map**. Contour means "shape," and a contour map shows the shape of a land surface. In reality contour maps have some similarities to elevation maps. They show ranges of elevation, but instead of using colors, they use lines and numbers. You can see this clearly on the contour map below.

- Find Cadillac Mountain on the contour map. It is the highest point along the East Coast of the United States.

- Compare the way this map shows Cadillac Mountain to the elevation map on page 15. Both maps will show you that Cadillac's peak elevation is 1,500 feet. The elevation map shows that through color and the map key. The contour map shows you that because the highest contour line is labeled 1,500 feet. A **contour line** is a line on the map connecting points of equal elevation.

- Contour maps are useful for showing the slope of the land. Where contour lines are spaced fairly far apart, the rise in elevation is gradual. Where they are spaced close together, the rise in elevation is steeper.

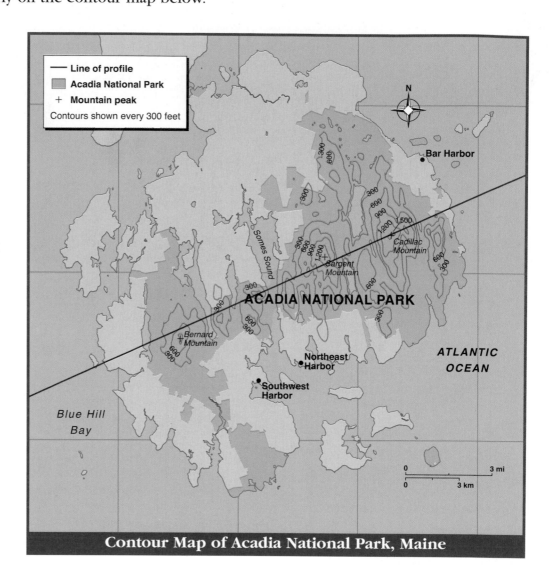

Contour Map of Acadia National Park, Maine

Somes Sound, Mount Desert Island, Maine

On Your Own

Use the information on pages 15 and 16 to help answer the questions.

1. What is the purpose of elevation maps and contour maps?

2. What do the different colors of elevation maps represent? How can you tell?

3. How is a profile of an area's elevation like a slice of cake?

4. On a contour map, what do contour lines show?

5. What do widely spaced contour lines tell about an area's land? What do closely spaced contour lines tell you?

Think Like a Geographer

6. Why is elevation usually measured from sea level?

7. Why would elevation and contour maps be important to airplane pilots?

8. Why would contour maps be useful to hikers and bikers?

9. What are the two different ways that Acadia National Park is shown on the two maps? In what situations might a geographer prefer an elevation map to a contour map? In what situations might he or she prefer a contour map?

Maps and Science

Mount Desert Island is made up of two peninsulas, which are separated by Somes Sound. This body of water is regarded as the only fjord in the eastern United States. Conduct Internet or encyclopedia research to define a fjord. Explain how fjords become part of Earth's surface, and where on Earth the major fjords are located. Draw a map to record your findings.

Climate, Elevation, and Land Use

Key Ideas

Elevation affects climate. Both elevation and climate affect how people use land.

Elevation and climate influence how people use the land. If you were to visit the long coast of the South American country of Peru, you would see farmers growing rice. If you went up to the highlands of the Andes Mountains, you would see people growing potatoes. Growing rice requires a warm climate while growing potatoes calls for a cooler one. Climates tend to get cooler as elevations get higher. Different kinds of maps and diagrams help us look at the way people use land.

- Peru lies close to the Equator. Its lower elevations have a warm tropical climate. This region is called *tierra caliente,* Spanish for "hot land." According to the chart, what crops are grown in this region?

- Find *tierra templada,* or "temperate land." What is its elevation? Name the crops grown here.

- Find the zone called *tierra fría,* or "cold land." What is its elevation? What crops are grown here?

Elevation (feet)

Elevation (meters)

TIERRA FRÍA

wheat   corn   potatoes
sheep   llamas

6,000 — 1,800

TIERRA TEMPLADA

wheat   corn   coffee   cattle

3,000 — 900

TIERRA CALIENTE

rubber trees   sugarcane
cacao   cotton   rice

Sea level — Sea level

Elevation Zones in Peru

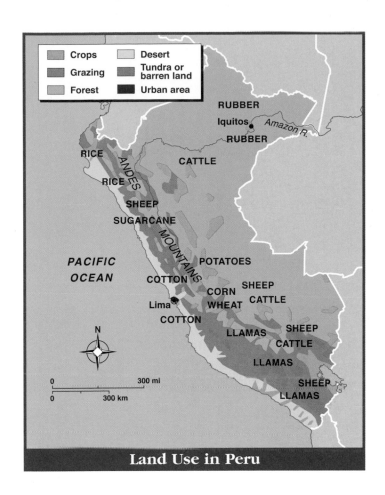

Land Use in Peru

Legend:
- Crops
- Grazing
- Forest
- Desert
- Tundra or barren land
- Urban area

- This is a land-use map. The term **land use** refers to the way people use land—for example, growing different kinds of crops, raising animals, manufacturing, and mining.

- Compare this map with the chart showing elevation zones. In which zone is Lima? Why is this a good location?

- Find the Andes Mountains on the map. In which of the three climate zones are they located? What examples of land use help you identify their elevation zone?

- Find the area on the land-use map where rubber trees are grown. In what elevation zone does it lie?

On Your Own

1. Explain how the <u>tierra fría</u> differs from the <u>tierra caliente</u> in elevation and in climate.

2. Why would it be difficult to grow cotton in the Andes Mountains?

Think Like a Geographer

3. Would you expect to find a wheat farm next to a rice farm in Peru? Why or why not?

4. If Peru did not have any mountains, what kind of climate would you expect it to have? Remember its location!

Maps and Economics

The potato is native to the Peruvian Andes and was unknown to the rest of the world 500 years ago. Research how it was introduced to other continents. Write a paragraph explaining its "discovery." Draw a map that shows which countries it went to from Peru.

Potato farming in the highlands of Peru

6 Nile River Valley, Then and Now

Key Ideas

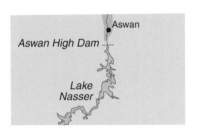

Maps can show people's relationship to the environment, both in the past and the present.

"The Gift of the Nile."

That is what the ancient Greek historian Herodotus called Egypt 2,500 years ago. Most of Egypt's land—in ancient times as well as today—is parched desert. But the fertile shores of the Nile River gave life to a desert region and helped Egyptians create one of the world's earliest civilizations.

Today, the population of the nation of Egypt is about 65 million and growing fast. Then and now, nearly all Egyptians live in the Nile River Valley. Using maps, we can compare ancient and modern Egypt. We can see how some people used the river thousands of years ago—and how people use it today.

This satellite image shows just part of the long course of the Nile River as it flows from southern Egypt to the Mediterranean Sea.

The Nile River Valley in Ancient Times

Egypt's farmers depended on the springtime flooding of the Nile River. Each year, far to the south, melting mountain snows and spring rains raised the river's level and sent millions of gallons of water, loaded with fertile silt, racing into Egypt. **Silt** is a mixture of fine sand, clay, and soil carried by water. When the flood waters were gone, the silt from the river was left behind as a new layer of rich, fertile soil.

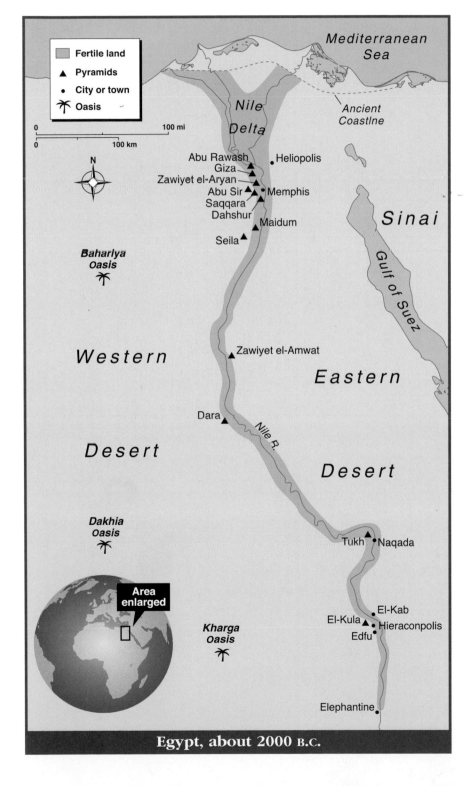

Egypt, about 2000 B.C.

- Note the shape of the map. It is more vertical—taller and narrower—than most maps in this book. Most ancient Egyptians lived and farmed in a narrow strip of fertile land along the Nile River.

- Find the fertile land on the map. It was also known as the "Black Land" because darker, richer soil was deposited there by flood waters. All that stretched to the east and west of it was sun-baked desert, the "Red Land."

- Find the Nile Delta. A **delta** is an area of land formed by deposits of silt as a river empties into the sea. Would you expect the delta to have good farmland?

- Compare this map to the image on page 20. Find the "Black Land," the "Red Land," and the delta.

- Use the map to explain the location of ancient cities of Egypt and why these cities developed there.

The Nile River Valley Today

By the twentieth century, Egypt's rapidly growing population created
pressure to farm more land. In the early 1960s, Egypt built the monu-
mental Aswan High Dam. Standing over two miles wide and nearly 400
feet high, it collects Nile waters in a gigantic reservoir, the 300-mile-long
Lake Nasser.

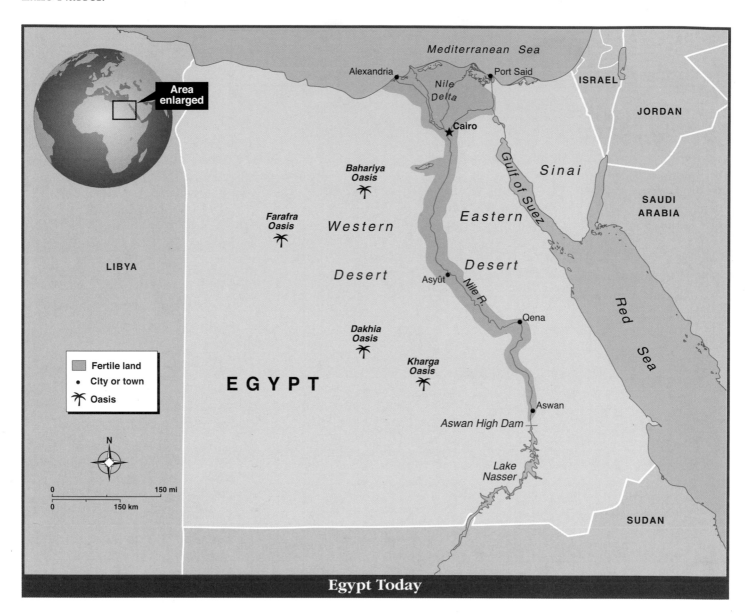

Egypt Today

- Look at the map of Egypt today. Find the Aswan High Dam and Lake
  Nasser. They are part of a huge irrigation system that has enabled
  more of Egypt's land to be farmed all year long. **Irrigation** is the bringing of water to dry land.

- Locate the Nile Delta on both maps. What major cities does today's
  map show there? At least 75 percent of Egypt's population lives in
  the delta region today. Why is this such a populated area?

The Aswan High Dam created Lake Nasser by damming up the waters of the Nile. The ancient monuments of Abu Simbel can be seen in the photograph. These massive statues had to be moved to higher ground to escape the rising waters of the new lake.

On Your Own

Use the information on pages 21 and 22 to help answer the questions.

1. How was the Nile River a "gift" to Egypt?

2. How was the Nile Delta created?

3. What ancient site is closest to Cairo— the capital city of Egypt?

4. In what part of Egypt is the Aswan High Dam located?

5. What new feature did it create? Do you consider this a human or physical feature? What are the reasons for your answer?

6. How did the Aswan High Dam make millions more acres of desert land available for farming?

Think Like a Geographer

7. Why might the Nile River have served as a "highway" running the length of Egypt in ancient times? Do you think that it is still a major route of transportation today?

8. The Aswan High Dam has had many positive effects on modern Egypt. However, it also has created negative effects. Huge amounts of land are now under the waters of Lake Nasser. Why would this be a problem?

Field Study

The Aswan High Dam, like all irrigation projects, is an example of the efforts of humans to modify their environment. Roads, buildings, jetties, and sea walls are other examples. In fact, countless human activities bring changes to Earth's surface. Take a walk around your neighborhood or community. What examples can you find of people altering their environment? Create a map with your findings.

Trade Routes and Early Civilizations

Key Ideas

Trade maps can show the routes used for the exchange of goods between ancient civilizations.

The ancient Egyptians used other natural resources besides the Nile River to develop one of the world's richest civilizations. The deserts beyond the river valley provided metals, such as copper, and granite, which Egyptians used for their huge building projects. But few tall trees grew in ancient Egypt, and the sparkling jewels worn by the kings and nobles could not be found there.

How did Egyptians get the resources their lands lacked? Just as we do today, people throughout history have traded. The trade map below shows the resources of ancient civilizations and the routes that ancient traders traveled.

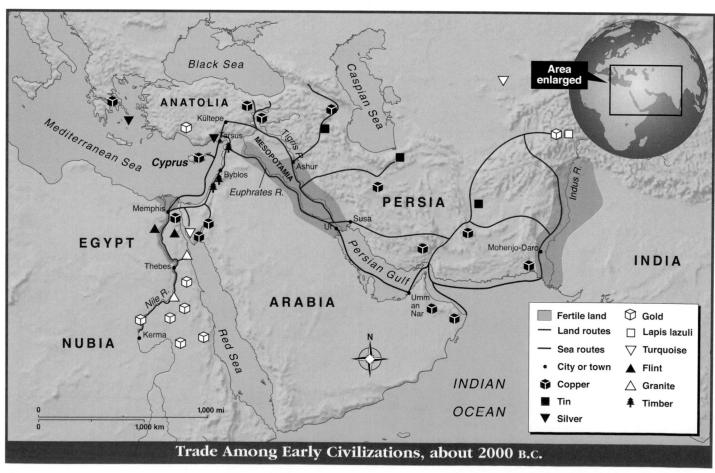

Trade Among Early Civilizations, about 2000 B.C.

- Like the Egyptians, other civilizations lived in fertile river valleys. Find Mesopotamia on the map on page 24. Along what two rivers was it located?

- Find the city of Mohenjo-Daro in the eastern portion of the map. Along what river was it located?

- Find the island of Cyprus in the Mediterranean Sea. It was an important source of copper, which early civilizations needed to make bronze. Describe the route used by traders to take copper to Egypt.

- The burial masks of the Egyptian pharaohs were covered with gold. Identify places where this valuable metal could be found.

From the tomb of Ti, a Fifth Dynasty official buried at Saqqara, wall reliefs provide a wealth of information on ancient Egyptian boatbuilding. Three vessels, portrayed under construction, are probably similar to working craft that sailed the Nile in Khufu's time.

On Your Own

1. Trace the trade route from Egypt to Mesopotamia. To what city along the eastern shore of the Mediterranean Sea would this route have taken traders?

2. From where and by what route would Mesopotamians have traded for tin? Timber?

3. Find Anatolia on the map. What resources were found there? Now find this area on the Atlas map on pages 70–71. What country is it today?

Think Like a Geographer

4. In ancient times, why were rivers important both to the development of civilizations and to trade among these civilizations?

5. As the map shows, the fertile river valleys of both Egypt and Mesopotamia were poor in mineral resources. What do you think these farming civilizations traded to get the minerals they needed?

Maps and Economics

Create and map your own trade routes! Find a product you use that comes from far away. Looking at maps, such as those in the Atlas on pages 66–71, write a description of the route your chosen product might have taken to get to you. Draw a map to go with your description.

Activity 8

Expansion of the Greek Empire

Key Ideas

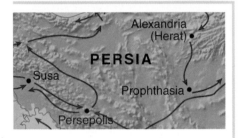

Historical maps can show changes in the borders and territories of a past civilization.

Time brings change, even to powerful civilizations like ancient Egypt. By 525 B.C., Egypt, along with most of its neighbors, had fallen to a new power from the East, the Persians. By 480 B.C., the Persian advance had been stopped by yet another emerging civilization—the Greeks. It was a young Greek king who began, in 633 B.C., a drive to conquest that created one of the largest empires the world had ever seen. That king would become known as Alexander the Great.

While Alexander's empire was vast, it did not last very long. As it broke up, other kingdoms took shape. How can we follow the shifting territories and borders that are so much a part of the world's history? One way is by studying historical maps.

The ruins of Persepolis mark the site of the ancient capital of Persia. After Alexander conquered the city, his army set it aflame and looted its riches.

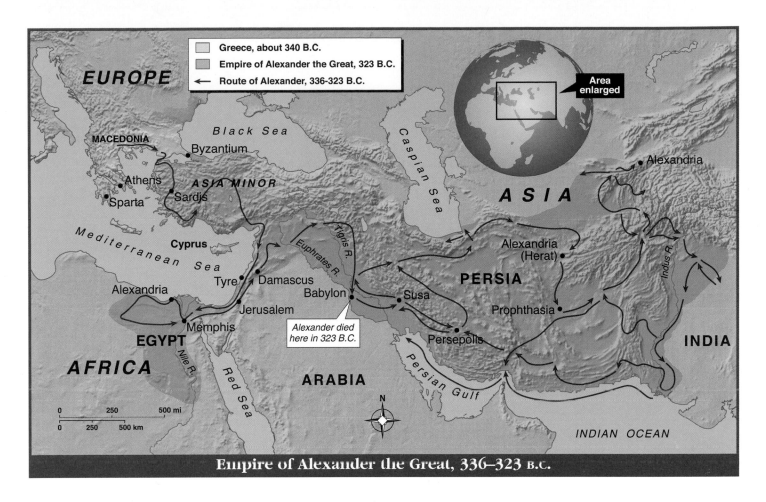

Empire of Alexander the Great, 336–323 B.C.

Map legend:
- Greece, about 340 B.C.
- Empire of Alexander the Great, 323 B.C.
- → Route of Alexander, 336-323 B.C.

Alexander died here in 323 B.C. (pointing to Babylon)

- Look at the map above. How does it help you compare the Greek lands before and after Alexander?

- Describe Alexander's route.

- Alexander founded a number of cities along his way and named them after himself. What evidence of this does the map provide?

On Your Own

1. Which bodies of water bordered Alexander's empire?

2. When did Alexander begin his path of conquest?

3. What was the farthest east he reached on his long march?

4. Where did Alexander end his period of empire-building? Why did it end?

Think Like a Geographer

5. Alexander's empire broke up shortly after his death. Why might his generals have had a hard time keeping control over so vast a territory?

Maps and Writing

Find the city of Byzantium on the map. It has had two other names since the time of Alexander. Find out what it was renamed. Why was its name changed twice? What is its name today? Write a paragraph in which you discuss your answers to these questions.

The Roman Empire: Comparing Map Scales

Key Ideas

A **large-scale map** shows more detail. A **small-scale map** shows more area.

The mighty Roman Empire reached its greatest size in A.D. 117. Throughout its huge territory was a network of well-built Roman roads. Along these roads traveled soldiers, military supplies, messengers, and government officials—a huge movement of people, goods, and information that made the empire function. "All roads lead to Rome," it was said, and many did.

Today, people move much faster on roads, but the purpose of roads is much the same as it was in Roman times. When we look at road maps, whether of ancient Rome or of modern highways, one of the most important elements of the map is its scale. A map's scale allows us to determine the distances between points. The larger the scale, the more detail a map can show.

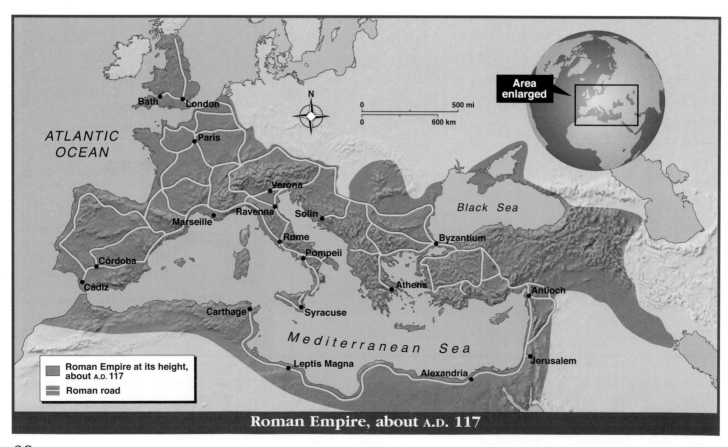

Roman Empire at its height, about A.D. 117

Roman road

Roman Empire, about A.D. 117

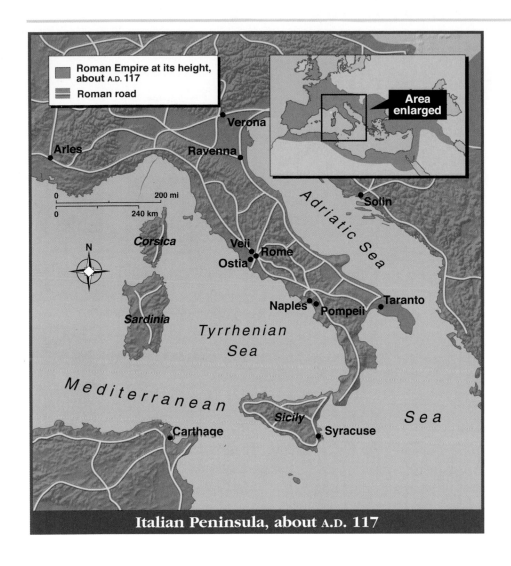

Italian Peninsula, about A.D. 117

- Look at the map on page 28. It has a map scale of 1 inch equals 500 miles and 2 centimeter equals 600 kilometers. Compared with the map on this page, it is a **small-scale map**. It shows a smaller amount of detail over a larger area.

- Look at the map on this page. What is its scale? Compared to the map on page 28, this is a **large-scale map**—one that shows a larger amount of detail over a smaller area.

- Compare the Italian peninsula on both maps. The small-scale map makes Italy appear smaller, and the large-scale map makes it appear larger.

On Your Own

1. Which map is drawn to a larger scale? Explain how you know.

2. What is the distance by road between Rome and Pompeii? Which of the two maps would give you a more precise answer? Why?

3. If you wanted to know the distance by road from Rome to Córdoba (today's Spain), which map would you consult? What is the distance?

Think Like a Geographer

4. Why are map scales necessary to make a map accurate?

Maps and Mathematics

Using the maps on these pages, choose three pairs of cities and write them down on a piece of paper. Then exchange papers with a partner and calculate the road distance between the cities of each pair.

Traveling the Silk Road

Key Ideas

Trade routes like the Silk Road linked different parts of the world, creating an exchange of ideas, cultures, and goods.

Two thousand years ago, it was so precious that giving away the secret of how it was made was punishable with death by torture. It was in demand from China, where it was made, to Rome, where only the wealthiest could afford to wear it. It was literally worth its weight in gold! This precious merchandise was silk, sometimes called the "Queen of Textiles."

Over the centuries a network of roads was developed to link China and Rome. The map shows the many routes that eventually became known as the Silk Road. Rugged terrain and cutthroat bandits were just two of its dangers. Yet traders traveled the Silk Road constantly, bringing silk to the West and wool, gold, and silver to the East. But it was not just goods that were exchanged along the Silk Road. It was also a route along which ideas, religions, and customs traveled between East and West.

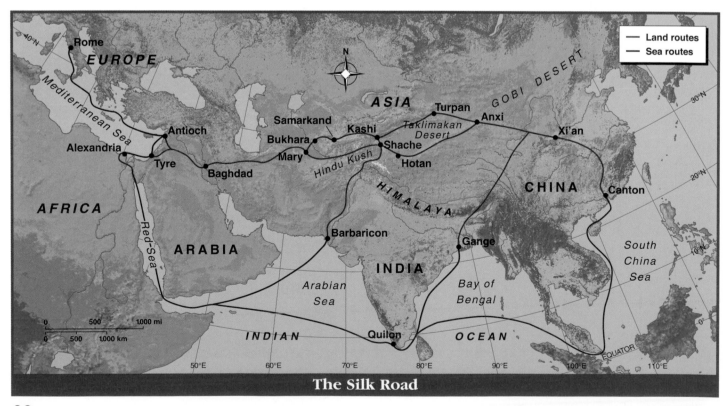

The Silk Road

- At first, most travelers journeyed by land, even though land routes were rugged and treacherous. Look at the map and find the land routes of the Silk Road. How are these routes shown on the map?

- By the 1400s, improvements in ships and sailing techniques opened sea routes, which were safer and easier. Find the sea routes on the map. How are these routes shown on the map?

- Travelers along the Silk Road helped to spread Buddhism from India and Islam from Arabia. Why were religions from these places likely to have been carried along the Silk Road?

- What physical features did travelers cross along the Silk Road?

On Your Own

1. What was the most eastern place on the Silk Road?

2. At what two places on the eastern Mediterranean shore did the land route end?

3. How was the last part of the trip from East to West made? Why do you think this route was used?

4. Use the map scale to measure the distance from Canton to Gange by land and by water. Which is longer? Why do you think the longer route was used?

Think Like a Geographer

5. Why do you think the Silk Road split into northern and southern branches at Anxi?

6. What role did the Silk Road have in the exchange of goods and ideas between China and other cultures?

NATIONAL GEOGRAPHIC
Map Fact

A Silk Road Sales Stop
Few traders traveled the entire 4,000-mile length of the Silk Road. Rather, a trader might travel in a caravan from Xi'an to Anxi, make a deal there with another trader, and then return to Xi'an. At each exchange, the price of the goods went up.

Consider This! How did the physical geography of the Silk Route contribute to making silk "worth its weight in gold"?

See NATIONAL GEOGRAPHIC magazine, "Silk—The Queen of Textiles," January 1984, pages 2–49.

The ancient ruins at Bezeklik, near Turpan in western China, were built by Buddhist monks in the fourth century along the northern fork of the Silk Road.

11 Winds and Currents

Key Ideas

A system of winds and ocean **currents** flows around Earth in regular patterns.

When Christopher Columbus first set sail from Europe west across the Atlantic Ocean in 1492, he was an experienced navigator. His lifetime at sea had taught him that winds consistently blow in certain directions at certain times of the year. He also knew that oceans contain **currents**, streams of water within the ocean, moving at a higher speed than the waters alongside them. Like other veteran sailors, he had learned to use winds and currents to help speed his sailing ships along. But he knew nothing about the winds and currents far out in the Atlantic where he was headed. No one had ever recorded them.

Though he did not know it at first, the wind-and-current system he encountered during his first voyage helped him both ways across the Atlantic. On his second voyage, he made sure to follow it again. The map below shows trade winds and currents in the Atlantic Ocean. Modern-day ocean navigators follow similar maps.

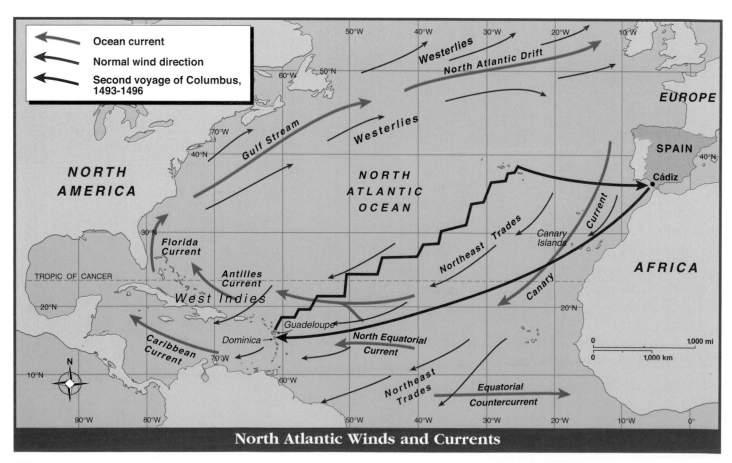

North Atlantic Winds and Currents

- The map on page 32 shows the pattern of winds and currents in the North Atlantic Ocean. Such patterns exist in all oceans.

- On the map, find the Westerlies. Winds are named for the direction from which they blow, not to which they blow. From what direction do the Westerlies blow? To what direction? Find the Northeast Trade Winds. To what direction do they blow?

- Find the major currents flowing from east to west. What are they? Find the major currents flowing from west to east. What are they?

On Your Own

1. From where did Columbus begin his second voyage?

2. In what direction did he sail?

3. What currents and winds must have moved his ship as he sailed west?

4. What winds challenged his return trip?

Think Like a Geographer

5. Other European sailors had tried to sail far into the Atlantic before Columbus, but they sailed from farther north than he did and they failed. What might have halted their progress to the west?

6. How do you suppose Columbus's navigational discoveries helped oceangoing sailors after him?

Maps and Science

The natural forces of winds and currents affect climate patterns on land. For example, the Gulf Stream brings relatively warm weather to the British Isles. Research the Internet or an encyclopedia to find out about one of the following currents or wind patterns and its effects on a region's climate: the Gulf Stream, the Jet Stream, the Northeast Trade Winds, the Peru Current, the California Current, the Alaska Current, the East Australia Current, or the West Australia Current. Write a brief report of your findings and include a map.

On his first voyage west in 1492, Columbus sailed with a fleet of three ship—the *Santa María*, the *Niña*, and the *Pinta*. A reconstruction of the *Santa María* is pictured below.

12

Mapping a London Epidemic

Key Ideas

Maps can be critical tools in solving problems.

In 1854, in a single ten-day period, 500 people suddenly died in London, England. And they all died of the same illness in a single section of the city. The cause of death was determined to be cholera, a severe infectious disease of the small intestine. What was the source of this disease? How was it spreading? A physician named John Snow was determined to find out.

Dr. Snow began by drawing a map of the afflicted part of the city, a district called Soho. On this map he marked the home of each victim with a dot. This produced a map similar to the one shown on the left below. Thinking that drinking water might be carrying the deadly germs, he drew a map of the pumps that supplied Soho's drinking water. This produced the map on the right below.

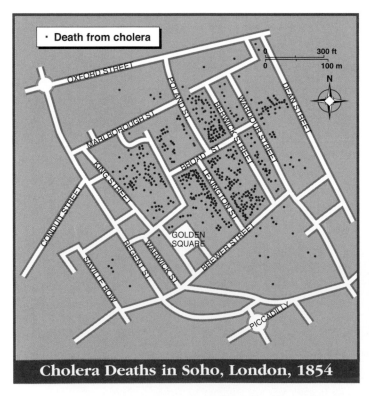

Cholera Deaths in Soho, London, 1854

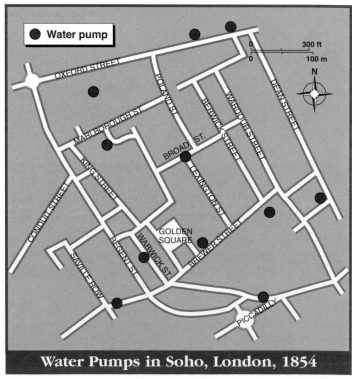

Water Pumps in Soho, London, 1854

- Look at the map on page 34 showing cholera deaths. What pattern do you see?
- Now look at the map showing water pumps. Which one do you think had the cholera-infected water? Why?

- How does putting together the information from these two maps help explain what happened? Dr. Snow convinced the London authorities to turn off the suspected pump. The number of cholera deaths immediately declined, almost to zero.

On Your Own

1. How did Dr. Snow's findings offer evidence that the source of the cholera was infected drinking water?

2. How did the results of turning off the suspected pump offer final proof of his theory?

Think Like a Geographer

3. Why would Dr. Snow have combined the information on the two maps onto one map in presenting his findings to the authorities?

4. Why might cholera deaths have occurred among people who lived farther away from the "killer pump"?

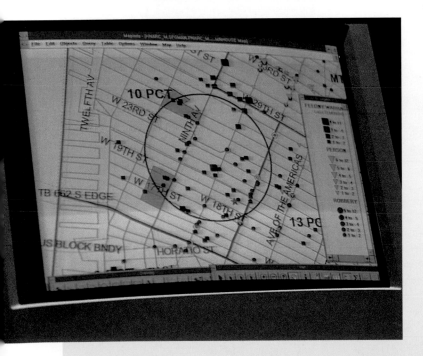

Crime Mappers

The New York City Police Department uses a method of mapping similar to Snow's to discover crime trends, but it uses more sophisticated technology. It is called Compstat, for computer statistics. An example is shown to the left. This system maps every crime that occurs in the city on computer and projects these computer maps on huge screens in a "war room." Police can spot clusters of similar crimes and then seek their source. Says one deputy police commissioner: "We don't solve any crimes in this room. But this is how we are able to manage our resources better and decide where and how to deploy our forces."

Consider This! Besides tracking information about crime, what other data might a city want to map?

See NATIONAL GEOGRAPHIC magazine, "Revolutions in Mapping," February 1998, pages 6–39.

Africa: Imperialism and Independence

Key Ideas

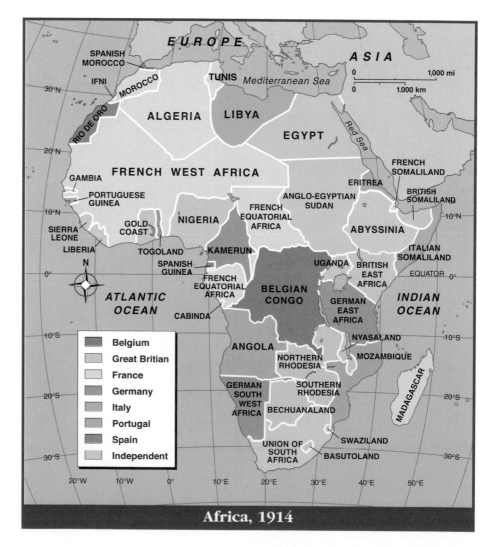

Political maps can show significant changes that result from conflicts among Earth's peoples.

Early historical records refer to the bustling island ports of Kilwa and Zanzibar. The mainland portion was called Tanganyika. Later, when European nations carved Africa into colonies, Germany declared it German East Africa. Later it was named Tanganyika again, and today it is called Tanzania. Same region—different names. But names are only a small part of the story. Africa, like all the world's continents, has seen tremendous political change over the years. Maps help tell the story of such change.

- This map shows the period of imperialism, when European nations had conquered most of Africa.

- Match the colors on the map to the map key. Which three nations held the most land in Africa?

- Which three African nations were independent in 1914?

Africa, 1914

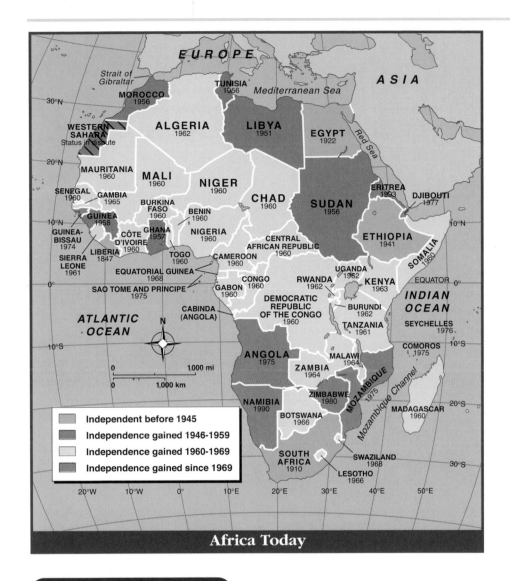

Africa Today

Map legend:
- Independent before 1945
- Independence gained 1946–1959
- Independence gained 1960–1969
- Independence gained since 1969

Countries and dates shown on map:
MOROCCO 1956, WESTERN SAHARA Status in dispute, ALGERIA 1962, TUNISIA 1956, LIBYA 1951, EGYPT 1922, MAURITANIA 1960, MALI 1960, NIGER 1960, CHAD 1960, SUDAN 1956, ERITREA 1993, DJIBOUTI 1977, SENEGAL 1960, GAMBIA 1965, BURKINA FASO 1960, BENIN 1960, GUINEA 1958, GUINEA-BISSAU 1974, CÔTE D'IVOIRE 1960, GHANA 1957, NIGERIA 1960, CENTRAL AFRICAN REPUBLIC 1960, ETHIOPIA 1941, SOMALIA 1960, SIERRA LEONE 1961, LIBERIA 1847, TOGO 1960, CAMEROON 1960, EQUATORIAL GUINEA 1968, SAO TOME AND PRINCIPE 1975, GABON 1960, CONGO 1960, RWANDA 1962, UGANDA 1962, KENYA 1963, DEMOCRATIC REPUBLIC OF THE CONGO 1960, BURUNDI 1962, TANZANIA 1961, SEYCHELLES 1976, CABINDA (ANGOLA), ANGOLA 1975, ZAMBIA 1964, MALAWI 1964, MOZAMBIQUE 1975, COMOROS 1975, NAMIBIA 1990, ZIMBABWE 1980, BOTSWANA 1966, MADAGASCAR 1960, SOUTH AFRICA 1910, SWAZILAND 1968, LESOTHO 1966

- Look at the map on this page, a political map showing Africa today. A **political map** shows governmental divisions such as countries, states, or provinces. What is the purpose of the different colors on this map? To what do the dates under each country's name refer?

- Compare this map with the one on page 36. What major change has occurred that causes the two maps to be different?

- Find Djibouti on the map of Africa today. What was it called under imperialism?

- Find French Equatorial Africa in 1914. Into what nations has it been divided?

On Your Own

1. How have the borders of Egypt changed between 1914 and today?

2. How has control over Nigeria changed from 1914 to today?

3. What is the name of German Southwest Africa today?

4. What are Northern and Southern Rhodesia called today?

Think Like a Geographer

5. Of the time periods on the map, in which years did the most nations win independence?

6. Look at the present-day map of Africa. Which countries do not have access to an ocean? What challenges does this present for these countries?

Field Study

Contact your local Board of Education. Ask for copies of current and past school boundary maps. How have the boundary lines changed over time? Why have they changed or not changed? Who determines where these lines are drawn, and why?

World Time Zones

Key Ideas

Time zone maps show differences in time anywhere on Earth.

Suppose that you wake up on the island nation of Fiji in the Pacific Ocean and you reach for the morning newspaper. If it is the *Fiji Times,* you will see that it proclaims itself "The First Newspaper Published in the World Today." It makes this claim because about one century ago, Earth was divided into 24 time zones, one for each hour in the day. The time zone just west of longitude 180°, the **International Date Line**, was picked to mark the start of each day. And Fiji lies right at that point.

Each 24 hours, Earth makes one complete rotation on its axis, turning 360°. Dividing 24 into 360 means that each time zone is about 15° wide. But as the map below shows, the width of some time zone boundaries varies, so that certain countries or regions can share the same time.

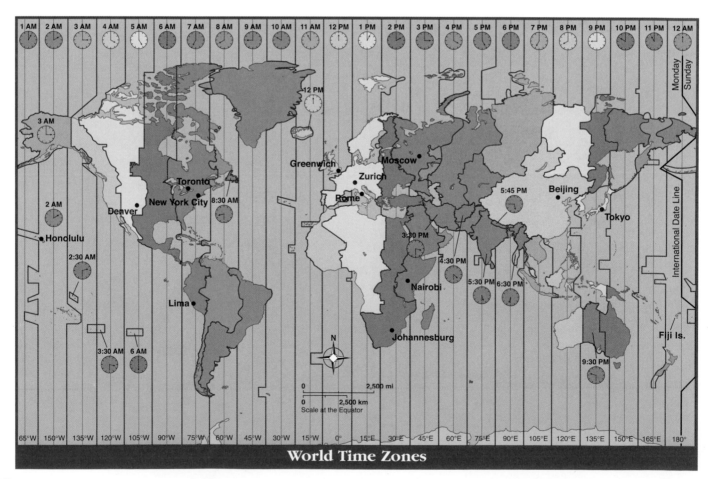

World Time Zones

- Time is counted from the prime meridian in Greenwich, England. Notice on the map that for each 15° of longitude you travel eastward, the time in most places is one hour later. For each 15° westward, the time in most places is one hour earlier.

- Find the International Date Line, at longitude 180°. If you cross this line from east to west, you move forward one day. If you cross it from west to east, you go backward one day.

- Note that the International Date Line does not always follow longitude 180°. Why is this? Find another example of a time zone border not exactly following its line of longitude.

On Your Own

1. Find the United States, including Alaska and Hawaii, on the map. How many time zones are there across the country?

2. How many time zones, or hours, separate New York City and Greenwich, England?

3. If it is 10 a.m. in New York City, what time is it in Greenwich?

4. If it is 4 p.m. in Moscow, Russia, what time is it in Nairobi, Kenya?

5. If it is May 2 just east of the International Date Line, what is the date just to the west?

Think Like a Geographer

6. What do you think were some of the reasons that people thought it was necessary to standardize time around Earth?

7. Think of one real-life situation that might cause someone to use a time zone map. What is it and how would a time zone map help?

Maps and Mathematics

Use a world time zone map to find three pairs of cities in different time zones. On a piece of paper, write down the three pairs of cities. For each pair, tell what time it is in one city and ask what time it must be in the other. Exchange papers with a partner and work out each other's problems. Then get together and check your answers.

City times around the world

39

15 World Cartogram

Key Ideas

A **cartogram** uses distortion in size and shape to show how countries compare with one another in different ways.

In geographic size, Japan is one of the world's smaller countries. It covers less land than the state of California. Yet on the map on this page, it appears as one of the largest countries. How can this be?

The map below is a cartogram. A **cartogram** does not attempt to show the relative geographic sizes of countries. Instead it distorts the countries' real size and shape to show how they rank with respect to something, in this case, how much wealth they produce. The amount of wealth a nation produces each year is called its **gross national product**, or **GNP**. The United States is shown as the largest country because it has the largest GNP. What can you conclude about where Japan ranks in the world in GNP?

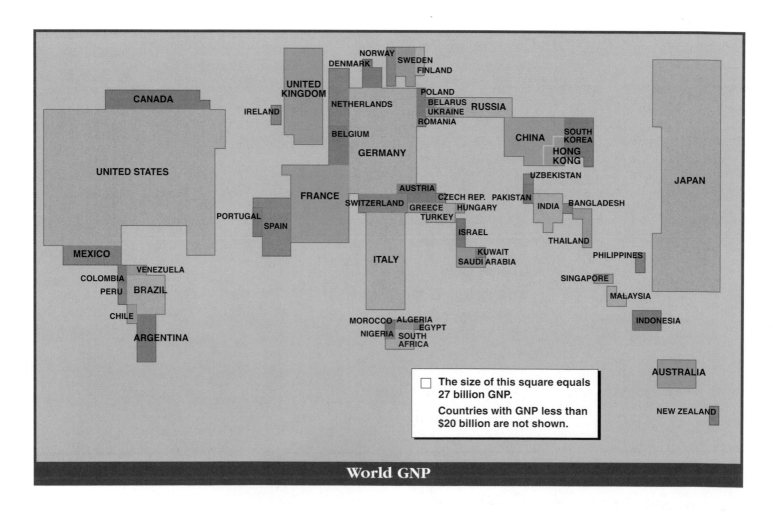

☐ The size of this square equals 27 billion GNP.

Countries with GNP less than $20 billion are not shown.

World GNP

- Note that the cartogram does not show the exact shapes of countries, but it does show countries arranged by their continents. The continents appear where you would expect them. Where is South America in relation to North America on the cartogram?

- Countries are drawn to scale on most other maps to show their actual land size in a smaller way. Cartograms are also drawn to scale, but this scale is proportionally based on the amount a country has of a certain item.

A bustling street in Tokyo, the capital of Japan

On Your Own

1. Based on the relative sizes shown on the cartogram, which country do you think has the fourth largest GNP in the world?

2. Which country in South America has the largest GNP?

3. Which has a larger GNP, India or Australia?

4. How do North Korea and South Korea compare in GNP?

5. Which country has the largest GNP in Africa?

Think Like a Geographer

6. Find Europe and Asia on the Atlas map on pages 70–71 and compare their sizes. Now compare their sizes on the cartogram. Which continent would you say has the largest GNP?

7. Find Africa on the cartogram. How would you compare the GNPs of African countries with those of European and Asian countries?

8. What other kinds of information would a geographer use a cartogram to show?

Maps and Economics

Suppose there is a small continent containing five countries—call it Continentia. Make up five names for its countries and assign a different GNP to each, for example, $3 trillion, $1.5 trillion, and so on. Then draw a cartogram of your Continentia, showing the relative sizes of its five countries, based on their GNPs.

16

Distribution of People and Resources

Key Ideas

	Forest region

Distribution maps show the pattern of how things are distributed, or spread out, on Earth's surface.

Earth is full of riches, but these riches are not equally shared by the world's countries. That is one conclusion that can be drawn from the cartogram in the previous activity. Cartographers create **distribution maps** to show the distribution of such things as natural resources, population, languages, and religions across the world.

● Thanks to satellite technology, it is now possible to map the distribution of warm and cold water on Earth. This satellite-generated image shows warmer ocean waters in reds and yellows.

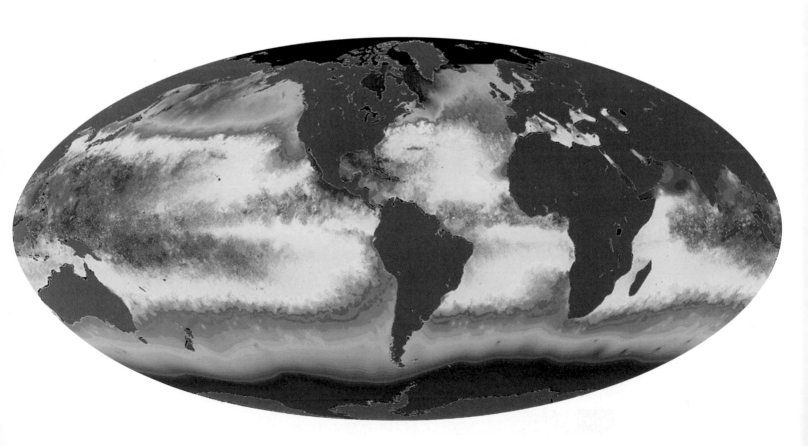

Using Resource Distribution Maps

The maps below show the distribution of two important natural resources, forests and oil. Forests are a **renewable resource**, one that can be replaced through natural processes. If you cut down a tree, a new one can grow in its place. Oil is an example of a **nonrenewable resource**. Oil deposits were formed millions of years ago, and once used up, cannot be replaced.

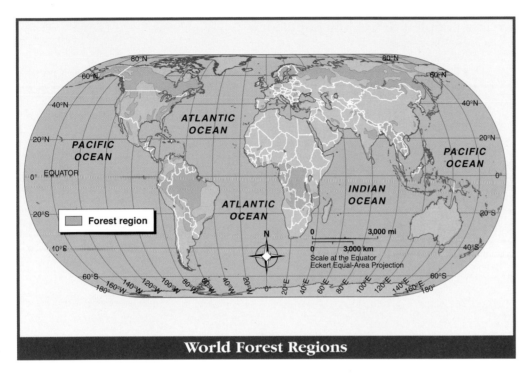

World Forest Regions

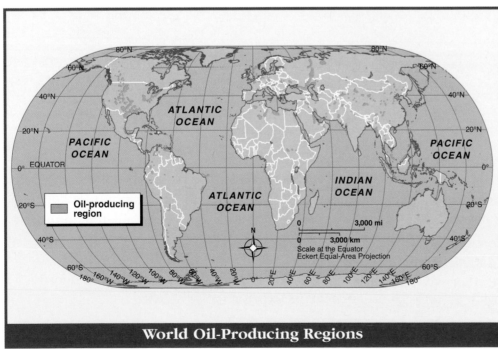

World Oil-Producing Regions

- Where are the major forest areas located in the Northern Hemisphere? How does this contrast to where forests are located in the Southern Hemisphere?

- Compare Australia's forest distribution with the forest distribution of the islands north of Australia. What do you notice?

- Where are the world's largest oil-producing regions? Why are these areas of great importance to the world?

- Find an example of a country or a region that has both oil and forests. What pattern can you find in the location of these two resources? Are they frequently found in the same region? Explain.

On October 12, 1999, the population of the world officially reached six billion. As the map below shows, people are far from equally distributed across the world. People tend to live in large numbers where the land is fairly flat, the soil fertile, the climate fairly moderate, and the rain adequate. Often this means river valleys and coastal areas. Geographers use the term **population density** to measure how heavily or lightly populated an area is. An area where many people live crowded together has high population density; an area where few people live has low population density.

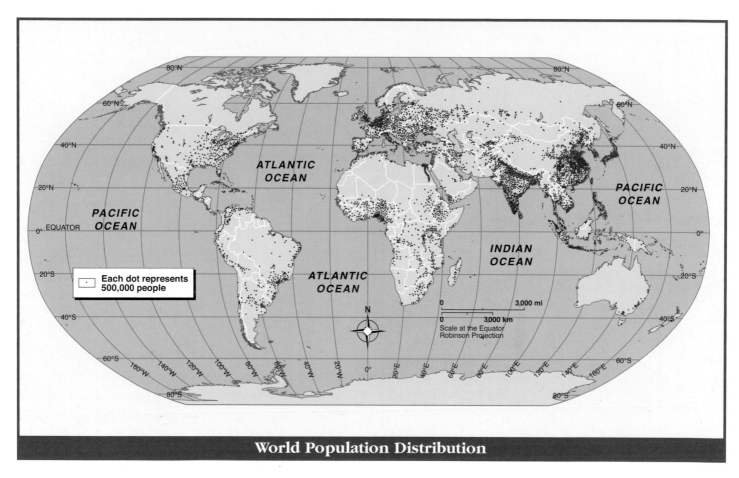

World Population Distribution

- Note that the map uses dots to indicate the location and numbers of people across the world. What does each dot represent?

- Find Asia on the map. It is the most heavily populated continent—more than 60 percent of the world's population lives there. Where are areas of high population density in Asia?

- Find Europe on the map. From the concentration of dots shown there, it might look like the second most heavily populated continent, after Asia. But in fact, Africa is the second most populated continent. How easy is it to estimate population from a population density map? Explain.

- Compare the forest distribution map and the population distribution map. Do forested regions support dense populations? Why or why not?

Use the information on pages 43 and 44 and the world political and physical maps on pages 68–71 in the Atlas to help answer the questions.

1. What is the purpose of a distribution map?

2. What does the term population density mean?

3. Find Brazil on the world political map on pages 70 and 71 and then locate it on the population distribution map. Describe the population density pattern you see.

4. What is the least populated area in Africa? Find this area on the world physical map on pages 68 and 69. Why might it be so sparsely populated?

5. Find Russia on the world political map and then locate it on the oil distribution map. Do you think it has more or less oil production than Europe? Explain.

Think Like a Geographer

6. How do you explain that population density decreases as you approach the North and South Poles?

7. Hundreds of years ago, nearly all of the eastern part of North America was forested. Why do you suppose that so much of northern Canada remains forested?

8. What continent has no oil producing region?

NATIONAL GEOGRAPHIC
Map Fact

Deforesting the Tropical Rain Forests

Look at the forest distribution map on page 43 and follow the Equator across it. Here are the world's tropical rain forests, so named because rain falls in them nearly every day. Edward O. Wilson wrote in NATIONAL GEOGRAPHIC magazine: "Like an undiscovered continent encircling the globe, tropical rain forests shelter an astonishing abundance of organisms—probably more than half of the earth's plant and animal species." Yet today these forests are being cut back at the rate of 55,000 square miles a year.

Consider This! Why are tropical rain forests located in a band of land around the Equator? Why are these forests so important to people everywhere in the world?

See NATIONAL GEOGRAPHIC magazine, December 1991, "Rain Forest Canopy: The High Frontier," page 84.

This section of rain forest in Indonesia was cleared by loggers.

United States Immigration

Key Ideas

Demography is the study of characteristics of human population. Maps can show patterns in demographic information such as immigration.

The United States has been called a land of immigrants, and so it continues to be. Today, one in ten residents of the country was born in another country. Each year, as many as 900,000 immigrants enter the United States looking for new lives. That is more than in any year since the early 1900s, when immigration reached its peak. At that time and before it, most immigrants came from Europe, by choice, or from Africa, as enslaved captives. But since the 1960s, most immigrants have come from other parts of the world.

These immigrants arrived at Ellis Island, New York City, in 1905.

Immigration Map with Pictographs

The map below highlights the eight countries from which the most immigrants came to the United States in 1996. The map also uses **pictographs**, symbols in picture form which show quantity. The pictographs show the approximate number of immigrants who came from each of these countries.

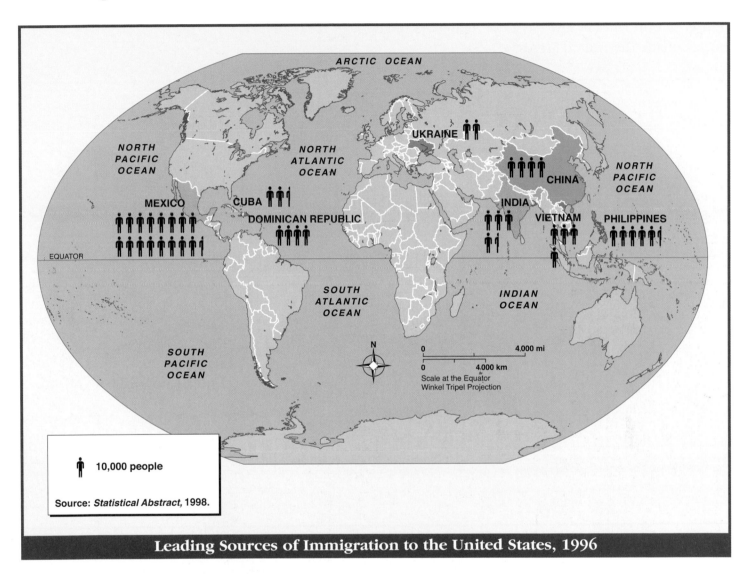

Leading Sources of Immigration to the United States, 1996

- Using the map key, find out how many immigrants each pictograph represents.
- From which country did the most immigrants come to the United States in 1996? On which continent is it located? How many immigrants came from this country?
- From which country did the next highest number of immigrants come? Where in the world is it located?
- From what four countries did similar numbers of immigrants come? How many came from each country?
- Find the only country in Europe that was among the top eight. What is it? How many immigrants arrived from there?

Maps and Demographic Information

About 25 million people who live in the United States were born in other countries. As you might expect from your map studies so far, immigrants are not distributed equally across the country. The map below uses pie charts to provide demographic information about immigrants in the United States. **Demography** is the study of characteristics of human populations, such as age, gender, and birthplace. The states highlighted on the map below have the highest percentage of residents born outside the United States.

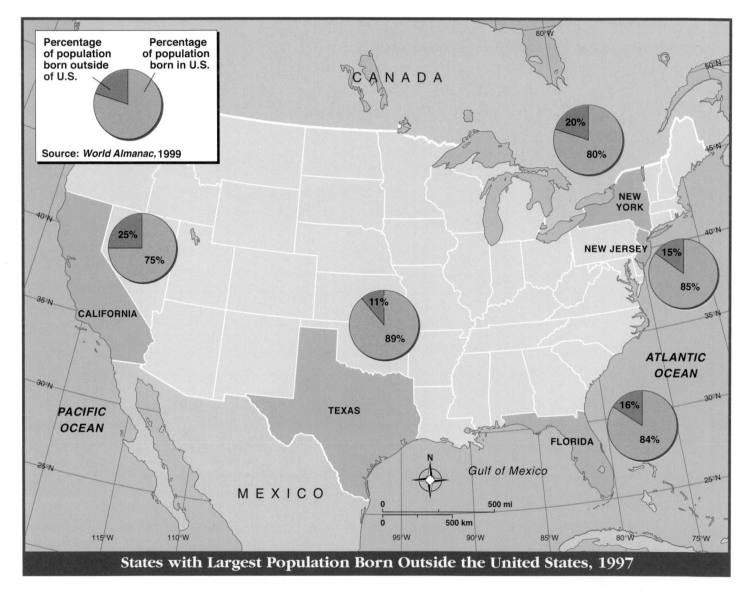

States with Largest Population Born Outside the United States, 1997

- Find Texas and study the pie graph associated with it. What is the percentage of Texas residents born outside the United States?

- Identify the state that has the highest percentage of residents born outside the country.

- Review the location of each of the highlighted states. Can you find anything that these locations have in common that might cause these states to have a higher percentage of people born outside the United States?

Use the information on pages 47 and 48 to help answer the questions.

1. Which country shown ranks last as a source of immigrants to the United States?

2. How many immigrants came from this country in 1996?

3. Which of the leading sources of U.S. immigration are island nations?

4. Compare immigration to the United States from Mexico and Ukraine. What is the ratio of Mexican immigration to Ukrainian immigration?

5. Which state has the second highest percentage of residents born in other countries?

6. Which state's population of residents born outside the country falls in the 10–14% range? What major source of U.S. immigration does it border?

Think Like a Geographer

7. Florida has a high number of residents born outside the country. Look at the area off the coast of southern Florida. Where do you think that some of these residents were born? Why?

8. What evidence can you find to support the statement that the sources of immigration to the United States have changed since 1900?

Map Fact

Chain Migration

Because United States immigration law gives priority to relatives of immigrants, "chain migration" has developed. A pair of immigrants arrives legally and begins to build a life, finding a job and a home. Then they sponsor another relative or two to come and join them. In one fairly typical case, over time, a single set of grandparents sponsored a total of 12 children and their spouses, as well as their grandchildren.

Consider This!

Suppose you could project the map on page 47 into the future. How might chain migration affect the percentage of United States residents born in other countries ten years from now? Fifty years from now?

See NATIONAL GEOGRAPHIC magazine, "Immigration Today: New York's New Immigrants," September 1990, pages 103–105.

On May 17, 1996, 300 new immigrants were sworn in at naturalization ceremonies on Ellis Island in New York City.

Trade Along the Pacific Rim

Activity 18

Key Ideas

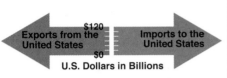

Trade maps can show volume and direction of trade around the world.

Hong Kong Harbor

It is 1945 and World War II has just ended. Countries around the western rim of the Pacific Ocean, several of them battlefields in the war, lie in various stages of ruin. Japan's former industrial might has been bombed to rubble. The economy of China, a wartime victim of Japan, is also staggering. Korea has not only suffered in World War II, but will be torn apart again by war in the early 1950s.

Fast forward to the late 1970s. Japan has become a world leader in the manufacturing of cars, cameras, and television sets and is forging ahead in the new field of computers. It ranks near the top of the world's strongest economies. Four of its Asian neighbors—Taiwan, Hong Kong, Singapore, and South Korea—have pursued industrial growth so successfully that they are now known as the "Asian tigers." By the 1990s, these five nations, including China which took control of Hong Kong, are major trading partners of the United States. The map on the next page presents information about trade along the **Pacific Rim**—nations that border the Pacific Ocean—a region in which trade is becoming increasingly important.

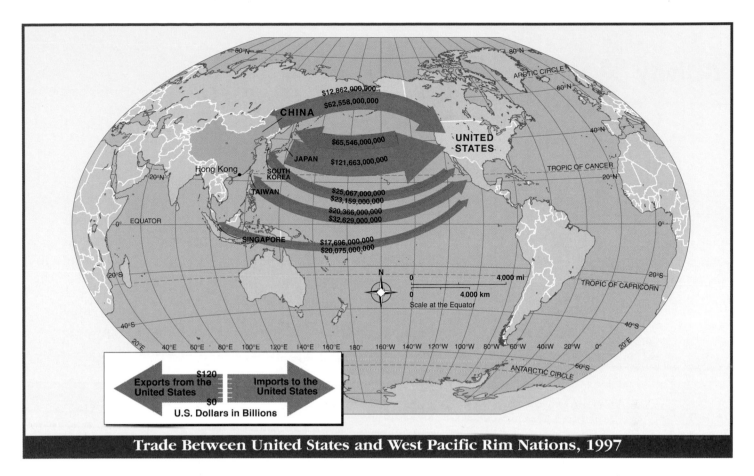

Trade Between United States and West Pacific Rim Nations, 1997

- Look at the map key. How does it distinguish between imports and exports? How does it track the directions in which trade moves?

- Find the vertical scale in the map key. How does it show volume, or the dollar amounts, of trade?

- Which country had the most exports to the United States? The most imports from the United States?

On Your Own

1. Of the countries shown, which one exported the least to the United States? Which imported the least from the United States?

2. To which nation did the United States export more, Singapore or China?

3. With which Asian country did the United States have the most total trade (imports and exports)?

Think Like a Geographer

4. Why is the world's ocean system so important to the trade of the Pacific Rim nations?

5. With which nation did the United States export more than it imported? Why might this be beneficial to the American economy?

Maps and Economics

Canada and Mexico are two of the leading trading partners with the United States. Do some research on the Internet or in almanacs to find statistics for Canada—U.S. trade and Mexico—U.S. trade. Then draw a trade map, similar to the one on this page, that shows the direction and volume of trade between the United States and these two nations.

19 Urban Regions

Key Ideas

Maps and satellite images can show the explosive urban growth that the world is experiencing.

In 1950, seven urban centers in the world had populations larger than five million. By 1995, there were 14 urban centers with more than 10 million people each. The growth of larger and larger cities will be one of the major challenges facing people in the twenty-first century.

The satellite image below was put together using many smaller images to create a picture of the world at night. It shows city lights burning in urban regions across the world.

- To help you locate places shown on the image of the world at night, compare it with the United States political and world political maps on pages 66–67, 70–71 of the Atlas.

- Locate the concentration of city lights along the northeastern coast of the United States. What cities do they show?

- Locate the heavy concentration of lights along islands off the eastern coast of Asia. What country or countries do they show?

- Find the bright red lights around the Persian Gulf. Much of this light is from natural gas and oil burn-offs. Find other examples of bright red lights from oil and gas production.

- Some lights are offshore. Lights in the Sea of Japan are from fishing boats.

On Your Own

1. What urban region do the lights show along the southern part of the Great Lakes in North America?

2. Why do you think the world's urban centers are not distributed evenly on the Earth's surface?

3. What part of Australia is the most heavily populated?

Think Like a Geographer

4. Find the large unlit portions of South America and Africa and find them on the world physical map on pages 70–71 of the Atlas. Why would these areas have no urban regions?

5. Based on the satellite image on page 52, would you say that the British Isles are heavily urbanized? Why or why not?

Field Study

Work together as a class to make a nighttime image of your community. Start by finding a map of your community. Have your teacher or another adult create a large photocopy of the map. Then, by visiting sites or surveying members of the community, determine which streets and areas are well-lit at night—usually commercial streets and shopping centers will be brightest. Mark those areas on your map. Then use black construction paper to create a reverse image of the map. Use white or yellow paints or markers to show lights and street outlines.

Workers construct a new commuter train line in Jersey City, N.J.

Ocean Floor and Space: New Frontiers

Key Ideas

Maps can show the shape of hidden ocean floors and the vastness of space.

What lies beneath the oceans that cover two-thirds of Earth? What lies out in the universe that stretches endlessly into space? Since ancient times, these two great mysteries have challenged humankind.

Mapping the Ocean

Serious exploration of the deep ocean floor began only about 150 years ago. A major purpose for this exploration was the desire to lay communication cables through the sea, like telegraph wires across land. These explorations revealed that the terrain under the oceans is much like that on land. It is made up of mountain ranges, ridges, plains, valleys, basins, and rifts.

- High peaks and low valleys of the land under the ocean are shown by this computer-generated image. The shallowest waters are shown in red, followed by yellow, green, blue, and purple as the water increases in depth. Where is the largest area of deep ocean water located?

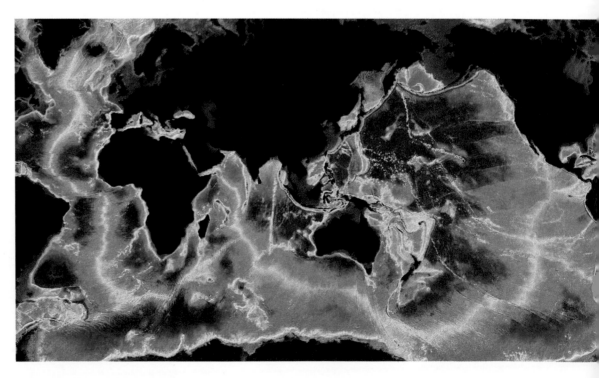

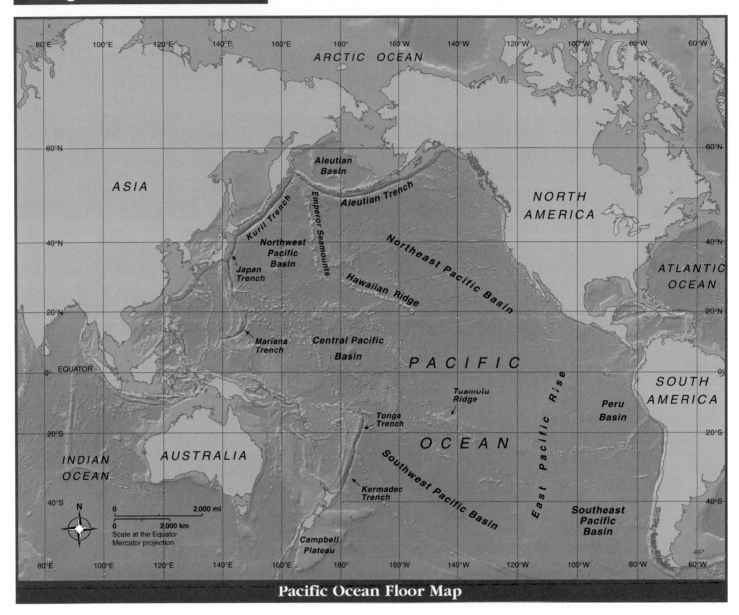

Pacific Ocean Floor Map

- Look at the image on page 54 and find the Pacific Ocean. Compare the Pacific to the way it is shown on the map above. As you can see, both the image and map show many of the same features.

- Locate the Hawaiian Ridge on the map. It was created by volcanic action beneath the ocean crust. The ridge became so tall that its peaks rose above the ocean surface, creating the Hawaiian Islands.

- Trenches are also shown on the map. These are the deepest parts of the ocean floor.

- Locate the Mariana Trench. It is the deepest point known on Earth's surface. It descends to a depth of more than 35,827 feet (10,920 meters), or nearly 7 miles (11 kilometers), below sea level. It is almost 7,000 feet (2,134 meters) deeper than the highest mountain on land, Mount Everest, is tall.

millions of miles

| 240 | 480 | 720 | 960 | 1200 | 1440 | 1680 |

Mars 141.6   Jupiter 483.6   Saturn 888.2   Uranus 1,786.4

Earth 93.0

Venus 67.2

Mercury 36.0

Mapping the Solar System

Mapping the solar system presents many challenges. People's abilities to explore space are limited, so our knowledge of space comes mainly from telescope observation. Because space is three-dimensional, a two-dimensional sheet of paper cannot truly show the positions of the planets in relation to each other. There is also the problem of scale. The distances of the solar system are vast. Pluto, the farthest planet, is about 100 times farther from the sun than Mercury, the closest planet. If you drew a map with Mercury about 1 inch (2.5 cm) from the sun, you would have to place Pluto 100 inches (254 cm), or more than 8 feet (2 m), farther! To show Pluto's oval orbit, you would need a sheet of paper almost 20 feet long (6 m). A diagram such as the one above can help us understand distances. It shows the average distance of each planet from the sun.

- This diagram displays its scale differently than most maps. It marks the entire length of the diagram to show the distances. Use a ruler to determine the distance that 1 inch (2.5cm) represents.
- Unlike distances, the sizes of the planets are not drawn to scale. Jupiter, the largest planet, is about 60 times larger than Pluto, the smallest. If the planet sizes were drawn to scale, Jupiter would take up nearly an entire page of this book.

- Next to each planet's name is its distance from the sun. How far is Earth from the sun?
- Locate the four inner planets—those closest to the sun. How far is each from the sun? Now find the five outer planets. How far is each from the sun?
- What is the distance between Mars and Jupiter? Between these two planets is an asteroid belt that measures about 150 million miles (241 million km) across.

Hubble Space Telescope

| 1920 | 2160 | 2400 | 2640 | 2880 | 3120 | 3360 | 3600 |

Neptune 2,798.8

Pluto 3,666.2

KEY
1" = 240 million miles

Note: To fit the inner planets, the first 240 million miles from the sun are not drawn to scale.

On Your Own

Use the information on pages 55–57 to help answer these questions.

1. How do trenches on the ocean floor differ from ocean ridges?

2. What ocean basin do the Aleutian, Kuril, and Japan trenches border?

3. What is the deepest point on Earth's surface? In which ocean is it located?

4. What rise divides the Southwest and Southeast Pacific basins?

5. How far is Earth from each of its two closest planetary neighbors?

6. How far is Saturn from its nearest neighbor?

Think Like a Geographer

7. Locate the East Pacific Rise on the map on page 55. From its name, how would you describe this area of the ocean floor?

8. You have read that Pluto is about 100 times farther from the sun than Mercury. Use information from the diagram to support this statement.

Telescope in Space

One of the most exciting space research tools that technology has developed is the Hubble Space Telescope, or the Hubble "eye in space." Launched by the space shuttle Discovery in 1990, it orbits Earth 370 miles up. Soaring beyond Earth's atmosphere, it has a clearer view of the heavens than the most powerful land-based telescope. It has provided the first clear pictures of the planet Pluto.

Consider This! Many observatories are located on mountain peaks, far from cities. Why would such a location be important to astronomers? How does the location of the Hubble Telescope take advantage of similar conditions?

See NATIONAL GEOGRAPHIC magazine, "The Hubble Telescope," April 1997, pages 2–17.

Create Your Own Map

You can use cartographic skills to draw a map of your own.

Suppose that you have been assigned to draw a map of a small area, such as your schoolyard, a park, or someone's backyard. To make an accurate map, you would measure the area's dimensions and show them in feet on the map, using a map scale. You would show cardinal directions by including a compass rose. How will you go about making these measurements?

Estimating Length or Distance

We have a measuring device with us at all times—**pace**, a measurement of two steps of a person's walking stride. Once you have determined the length of your pace, you can use it to estimate distances without the help of other measuring devices.

- I counted 40 steps when I walked the 100-foot distance.
- A pace is 2 steps, so 40 steps is 20 paces.
- Divide number of paces into the distance covered

100 divided by 20 = 5

My pace is 5 feet long.

- You will need a standard measuring device to start. Use a tape measure to measure a 50-foot (15 meters) distance outside or down a school corridor.

- Using your usual, comfortable stride, start off on your left foot to pace the known 50-foot (15 meters) distance in a straight line.

- Count a pace every time your right foot hits the ground (2 steps = 1 pace).

- Pace the distance twice, to cover a distance of 100 feet (30 meters).

- Now compute the length of your pace by dividing the distance covered by the number of paces you took. For example, if you counted 20 paces in 100 feet (30 meters), your pace is 5 feet long (1.5 meters).

Using a Compass

The **compass** is the basic tool used to determine direction. It works because of an amazing property of our planet. Earth actually behaves like a giant magnet! And like all magnets, Earth has two poles, north and south. A magnetic pole is the place on either end of a magnet where the magnetic forces are concentrated.

A compass has a needle mounted on a pivot, so that the needle can swing easily. The needle points to the magnetic north. Magnetic north is not exactly the same as true north—the direction to the North Pole—but it is very close. So the compass needle tells you the approximate direction of north.

- The face of a compass shows the four cardinal directions—north, south, east, west—and the intermediate directions—northeast, southeast, southwest, and northwest. Sometimes it shows other in-between directions as well.

- Find a compass. Hold it waist high. Be sure that no metal objects are nearby that might affect the compass reading.

- Hold the compass steady and turn your body until the arrow on the needle aligns with N (for north) on the compass. Now you are facing north. Directly behind you is south, to your right is east and to your left is west.

Field Study

Now you are ready to gather your map data and create a map from it.

Step 1

Make a preliminary sketch of the borders of your schoolyard. Then pace each border. Using the length of your pace that you have already determined, compute the length of each border. Adjust your sketch to show the actual scale. Draw a map scale in inches to show how the lengths of the lines you show relate to the actual lengths in feet of the borders.

Step 2

Stand in the schoolyard and use a compass to orient, or establish directions on your sketch. Mark the directions north, south, east, and west on your preliminary outline. Draw a map compass to show how your map relates to the cardinal directions.

Step 3

On your sketch, show objects of interest, such as trees, ball fields, and buildings. Use pacing to position them accurately. For example, if a tree stands several feet from the northern and western borders, pace the distance from each border to pinpoint the location exactly. Show each object with a symbol and make a map key that tells what the symbol represents.

Step 4

Review your map to make sure it is showing what you want, and that it is accurate. Now carefully draw your final map, incorporating all the data you have assembled. You might want to reorient the map so that north is at the top of the page.

BRYANT SCHOOL

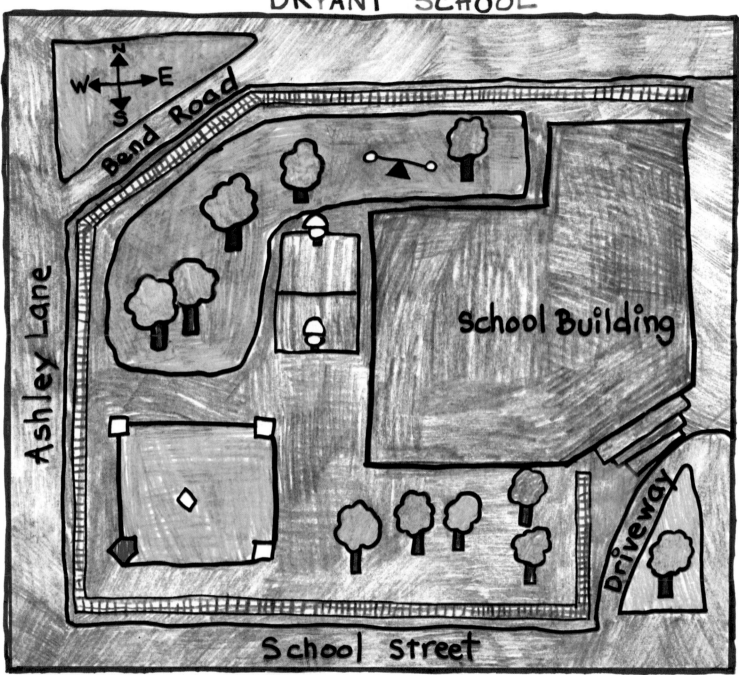

Bend Road

Ashley Lane

School Building

School Street

Driveway

KEY

- 🌳 Tree
- ▦ Fence
- ⌂ Basketball Court
- ⬠ Home plate
- ⟁ Playground

Scale
1 inch = 60 feet

60 ft   120 ft

Map Review

CHOOSE the correct answer to the following questions.

1. Which area of China has the steepest changes in elevation?

    A. the Southeast coast
    B. Northeast
    C. South of the Taklimakan Desert
    D. Gobi Desert

2. The Silk Road cuts through which ranges of elevations?

    A. 0–5,000 feet (0–1,524 meters) and 5,000–10,000 feet (1,524–3,048 meters)
    B. 0–5,000 feet (0–1,524 meters)
    C. 5,000–10,000 feet (1,524–3,048 meters)
    D. all of the elevation ranges

3. It is 3 p.m. Tianjin, China. What is the time in Greenwich, England? Use the map on page 38 to help you.

    A. 10 p.m.   **C.** 7 p.m.
    B. 7 a.m.   **D.** 9 a.m.

4. How many time zones does China cover? Use the map on page 38 to help you.

    A. 3   **C.** 2
    B. 1   **D.** 4

5. Chinese farmers generally grow rice at elevations of

    A. 10,000–15,000 feet (3,048–4,572 meters)
    B. 5,000 feet–10,000 feet (1,524–3.048 meters)
    C. 0–5,000 feet (0–1,524 meters)
    D. 0–10,000 feet (0–3,048 meters)

6. In China, barley is grown in a climate that is generally _____ the climate where soybeans are grown.

    A. colder than
    B. the same as
    C. warmer than

7. The population of China is most dense at what elevations? Use the map on page 44 to help you.

    A. 0–5,000 feet (0–1,524 meters)
    B. 5,000–10,000 feet (1,524–3,048 meters)
    C. 10,000–15,000 feet (3,048–4,572 meters)
    D. Above 15,000 feet (above 4,572 meters)

8. According to the satellite image on page 52, which city is the most urbanized area on China's mainland?

    A. Lhasa   **C.** Ürümqi
    B. Chengdu   **D.** Beijing

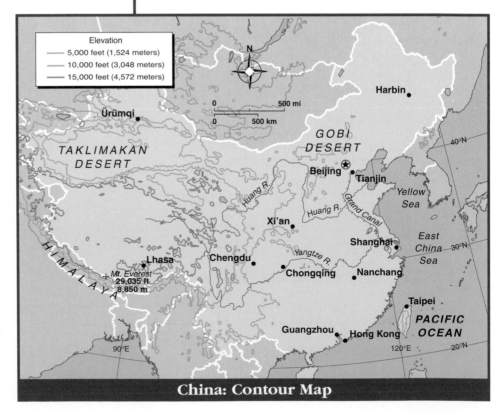

China: Contour Map

9. The Kuroshio Current is found in which body of water?

    A. North Atlantic Ocean
    B. South Atlantic Ocean
    C. North Pacific Ocean
    D. South Pacific Ocean

10. China is on what tectonic plate? Use the maps on page 11 to help you.

    A. Pacific Plate
    B. Eurasian Plate
    C. Indo-Australian Plate
    D. Philippine Plate

LOCATE the answer on the maps.

11. What is the distance in miles and kilometers from Shanghai to Mount Everest?

12. Name the bodies of water that are connected by the Grand Canal.

13. Name the elevation ranges where animals graze.

14. Which city has the following coordinates: 39° 56' N, 116° 24' E?

WRITE a paragraph that answers each question.

15. China's earliest civilizations developed in the Huang River Valley. Using what you know about the Nile River Valley, explain why and how early people may have lived along the Huang and what problems they may have encountered.

16. Does China import or export more goods to the United States? Does this benefit or hurt its economy? Why?

17. China produces more coal than any other nation in the world. If you were a cartographer, what type of map would you display this information on? Why?

18. Why do you think China's population is concentrated in the east?

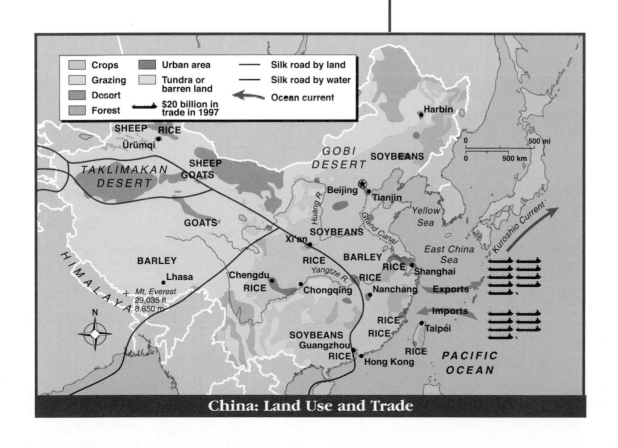

China: Land Use and Trade

Glossary

cartogram A map that distorts the size and shape of countries to show how they compare with one another in different ways. One purpose of a cartogram is to compare countries' gross national products (GNP). (page 40)

compass The basic tool used to determine direction. A compass works because of Earth's magnetism. (page 59)

continental drift The movement of tectonic plates. Continental drift causes plates to scrape past and collide into one another. (page 10)

contour line A line on a contour map connecting points of equal elevation. The change in elevation is steep when contour lines appear close together. (page 16)

contour map A map that uses contour lines to show the elevation of land. Contour maps and relief maps both show elevation. (page 16)

coordinates A set of latitude and longitude measurements that define a point on the global grid. Rescuers used the coordinates of Apollo 13's crash landing to find its crew. (page 4)

current A stream of water within the ocean that moves at a higher speed than the waters alongside it. Currents in the Atlantic Ocean helped Columbus on his voyage to the Americas. (page 32)

delta An area of land formed by deposits of silt as a river empties into the sea. A delta often has fertile land which is good for farming. (page 21)

demography The study of the characteristics of human populations. Age, gender, and birthplace are examples of characteristics studied in demography. (page 48)

distortion A change, or shift, in the natural size or shape of something. Cartographers try to limit the distortion of continents when mapping spherical Earth onto a flat surface. (page 6)

distribution map A map that shows the pattern of how a characteristic is spread out on Earth's surface. One characteristic a distribution map can show is population. (page 42)

global grid The pattern on a world map formed by intersecting lines of latitude and longitude. The global grid helps us locate points on Earth. (page 4)

Goode's projection A map projection that "interrupts" a world map near the Poles to correct size distortions. Goode's projection is a short way of referring to Goode's Interrupted Homolographic Modified projection. (page 7)

gross national product (GNP) Gross national product is the amount of wealth a nation produces each year. (page 40)

International Date Line The line of longitude, located at 180°, which marks the start of a new day. The International Date Line sometimes deviates from the 180° line so that certain countries and regions can share the same day. (page 38)

irrigation The bringing of water to dry land. Irrigation enables Egyptians to farm on lands that used to be desert. (page 22)

land use The way people use the land in an area. A land-use map shows how people use the resources in their area. (page 19)

large-scale map A map that shows a small area in a lot of detail. Compared to a small-scale map, a large-scale map makes places appear larger. (page 29)

Mercator projection Gerardus Mercator's projection of the world on a flat map, in which lines of longitude do not meet at the Poles. The Mercator projection has more distortion at the Poles than near the Equator. (page 6–7)

minutes Divisions of a degree of latitude or longitude. Sixty minutes equal one degree of latitude or longitude. (page 4)

nonrenewable resource A natural resource that cannot be replaced once it is used. Oil is a nonrenewable resource. (page 43)

pace The measurement of two steps of a person's walking stride. You can use your pace to measure distance. (page 58)

Pacific Rim The group of nations that border the Pacific Ocean. The Western United States is located on the Pacific Rim. (page 50)

Pangaea The name given to the "supercontinent." It existed 300 million years ago when all of the tectonic plates came together to form one continent. (page 11)

physical region An area that shares certain physical features, such as mountains or plains. The Himalaya mountains are an example of a physical region. (page 12)

pictograph A symbol in picture form used to represent data. A pictograph depicting a person could be used to represent the number of immigrants who came from a particular country. (page 47)

political map A map that shows governmental divisions such as countries, states, or provinces. Political maps can change over time as conflicts and agreements shift an area's borders. (page 37)

population density The measurement of how heavily or lightly populated an area is. An area where many people live crowded together has high population density. (page 44)

profile A view of something from the side. The elevation of a region can be determined by looking at its profile. (page 15)

projection The act of transferring images from one surface to another. Map projections show information from a globe on a flat surface. (page 6)

relief A mapping technique that uses shading to show differences in elevation. A map of a mountainous area shows more relief than a map of the plains. (page 12)

renewable resource A resource that can be replaced through natural processes. A forest is a renewable resource. (page 43)

silt A mixture of fine sand, clay, and soil carried by water. Silt left behind from Nile River floods provided the ancient Egyptians with fertile soil. (page 21)

small-scale map A map that shows a large area without showing much detail. Compared to a large-scale map, a small-scale map makes places appear smaller. (page 29)

tectonic plates Rigid pieces of Earth's outer shell. Several tectonic plates are large enough to include an entire continent. (page 10)

time zone (page 38)

Winkel Tripel projection A map projection that bends lines of longitude at the Poles in order to show Earth in correct proportion. The Winkel Tripel projection is an equal-area projection, meaning that it shows all regions of Earth in their correct relative size. (page 8)

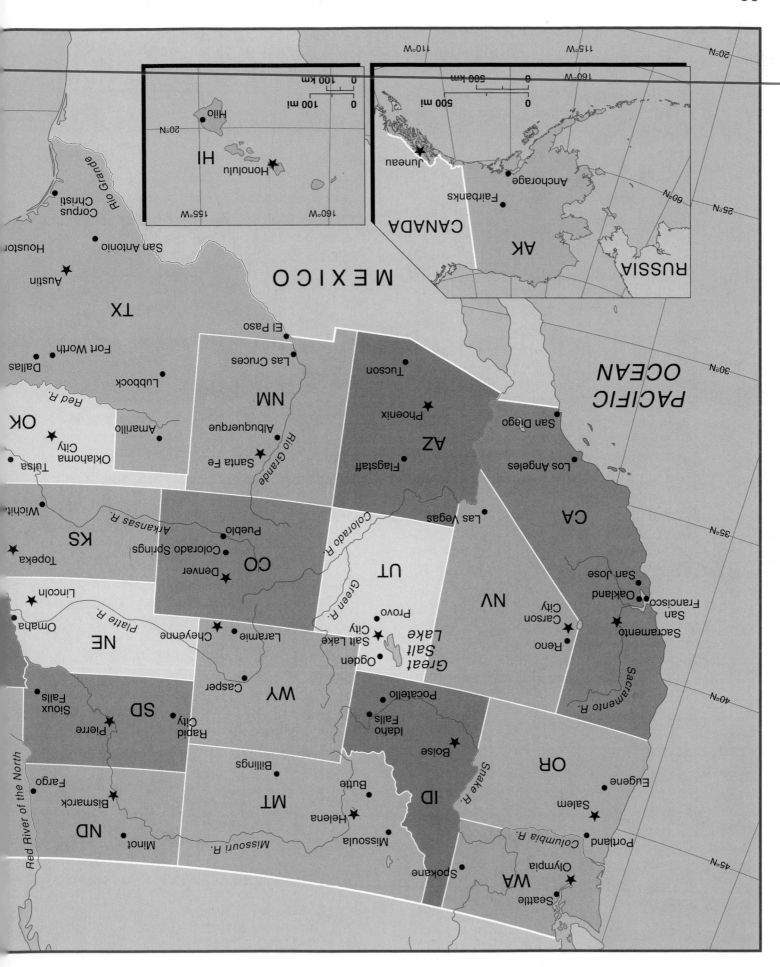

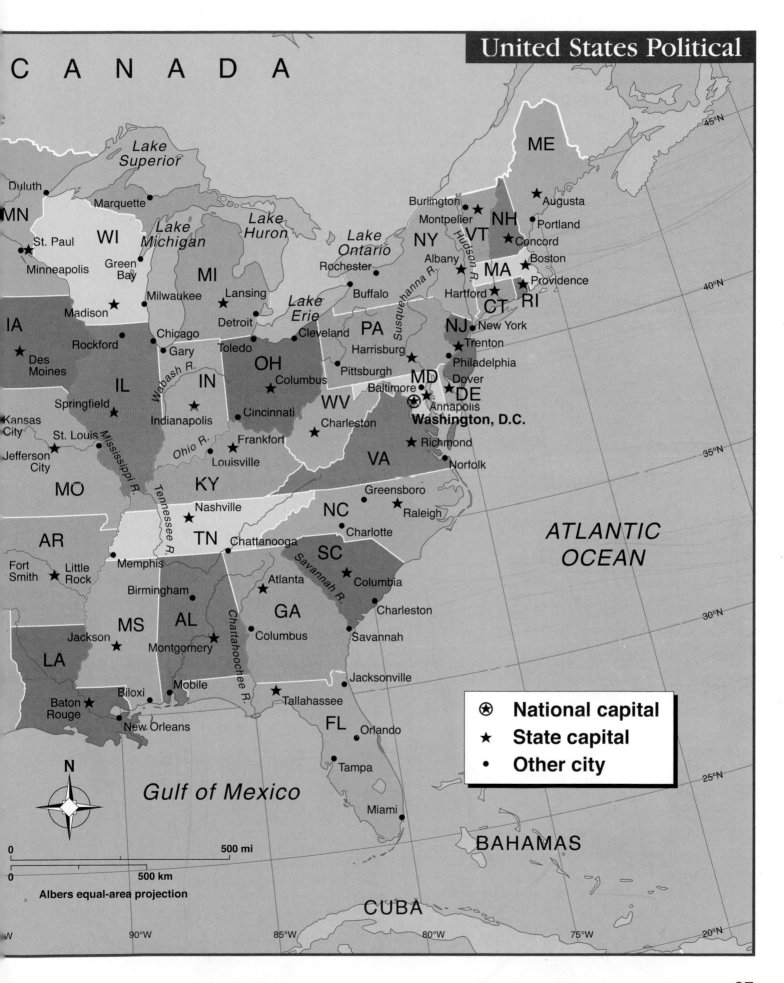

United States Political

CANADA

CANADA

Lake Superior

Duluth
Marquette

MN

St. Paul
Minneapolis

WI

Green Bay

Lake Michigan

Madison

Milwaukee

MI

Lansing

Detroit

Lake Huron

Lake Erie

Buffalo

Cleveland

PA

Lake Ontario

Rochester

Burlington
Montpelier

Augusta
Portland

ME

VT

NH

Concord

Boston

NY

Albany

Hudson R.

MA

Providence

Hartford

CT

RI

IA

Des Moines

Rockford

Chicago

Gary

Wabash R.

Toledo

OH

Columbus

Pittsburgh

Harrisburg

Susquehanna R.

NJ

New York

Trenton

Philadelphia

Dover

DE

Kansas City

IL

Springfield

Indianapolis

IN

Cincinnati

WV

MD

Baltimore

Annapolis

Washington, D.C.

St. Louis

Jefferson City

Mississippi R.

Ohio R.

Frankfort

Louisville

Charleston

Richmond

MO

KY

VA

Norfolk

Tennessee R.

Nashville

Greensboro

Raleigh

AR

TN

Chattanooga

NC

Charlotte

Fort Smith

Little Rock

Memphis

SC

Columbia

ATLANTIC OCEAN

Birmingham

Atlanta

Savannah R.

Charleston

MS

Jackson

AL

Montgomery

GA

Columbus

Savannah

LA

Chattahoochee R.

Biloxi

Mobile

Jacksonville

Baton Rouge

New Orleans

Tallahassee

FL

Orlando

N

Gulf of Mexico

Tampa

Miami

⊛	**National capital**
★	**State capital**
•	**Other city**

BAHAMAS

0   500 mi

0   500 km

Albers equal-area projection

CUBA

45°N

40°N

35°N

30°N

25°N

20°N

90°W   85°W   80°W   75°W

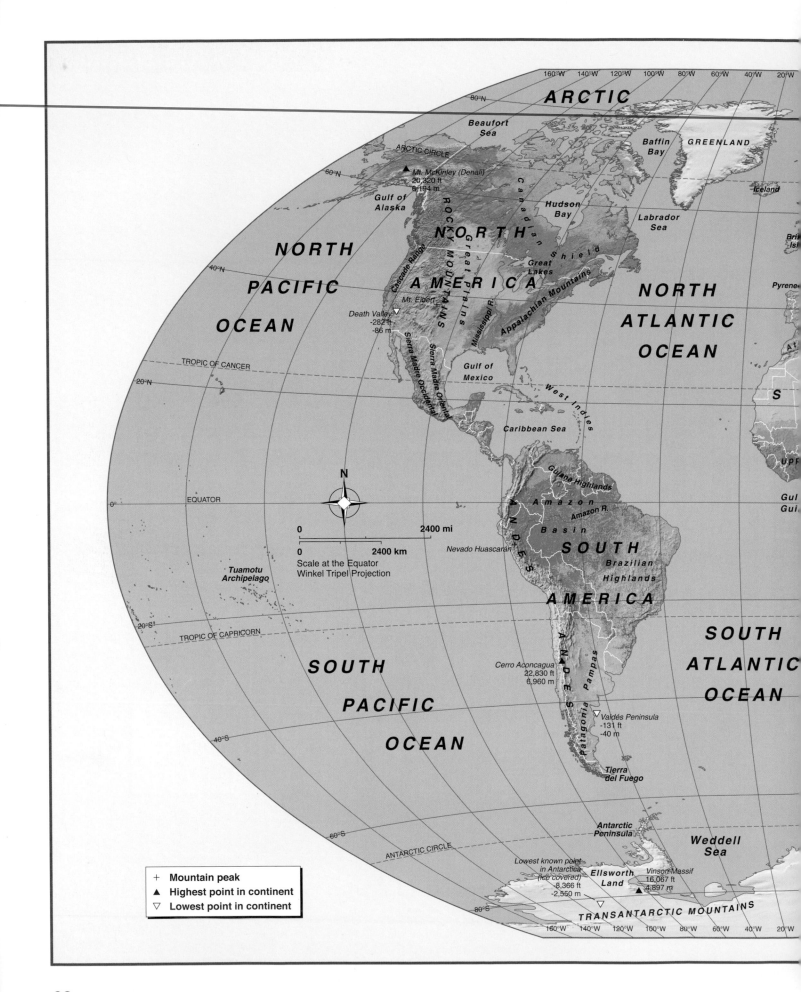

ARCTIC

North America / South America — Physical Map

North Pole region:
- Beaufort Sea
- ARCTIC CIRCLE
- Baffin Bay
- GREENLAND
- Iceland

- Mt. McKinley (Denali) 20,320 ft 6,194 m
- Gulf of Alaska
- Hudson Bay
- Labrador Sea
- Canadian Shield
- Great Lakes
- ROCKY MOUNTAINS
- Great Plains
- Cascade Range
- Mt. Elbert
- Death Valley -282 ft -86 m
- Sierra Madre Occidental
- Sierra Madre Oriental
- Mississippi R.
- Appalachian Mountains
- Pyrenees

NORTH PACIFIC OCEAN

NORTH AMERICA

NORTH ATLANTIC OCEAN

- TROPIC OF CANCER
- Gulf of Mexico
- West Indies
- Caribbean Sea
- Guiana Highlands
- Amazon Basin
- Amazon R.
- Andes
- Nevado Huascarán
- Brazilian Highlands
- Gulf of Guinea
- S

EQUATOR

N

Tuamotu Archipelago

0 — 2400 mi
0 — 2400 km
Scale at the Equator
Winkel Tripel Projection

SOUTH AMERICA

- TROPIC OF CAPRICORN
- Cerro Aconcagua 22,830 ft 6,960 m
- Pampas
- Patagonia
- Valdés Peninsula -131 ft -40 m
- Tierra del Fuego

SOUTH PACIFIC OCEAN

SOUTH ATLANTIC OCEAN

- ANTARCTIC CIRCLE
- Antarctic Peninsula
- Weddell Sea
- Lowest known point in Antarctica (ice covered) -8,366 ft -2,550 m
- Ellsworth Land
- Vinson Massif 16,067 ft 4,897 m
- TRANSANTARCTIC MOUNTAINS

Legend:
+ Mountain peak
▲ Highest point in continent
▽ Lowest point in continent

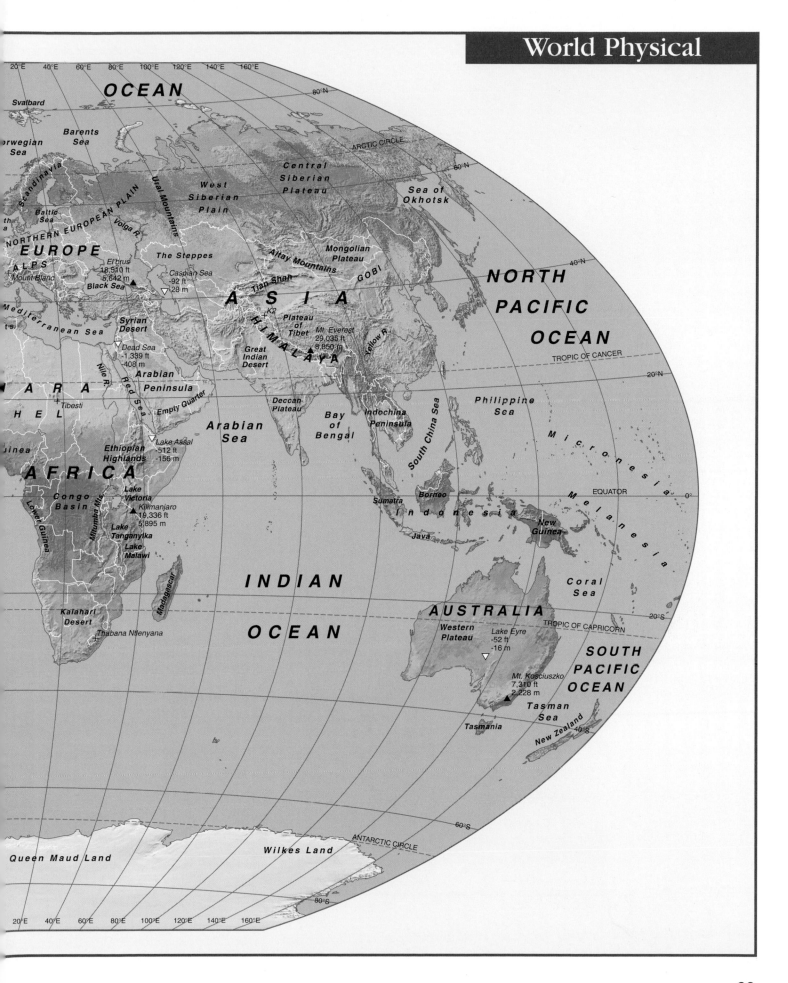

OCEAN

Svalbard

Norwegian
Sea

Barents
Sea

ARCTIC CIRCLE

80°N

60°N

Scandinavia

Baltic
Sea

NORTHERN EUROPEAN PLAIN

Ural Mountains

West
Siberian
Plain

Central
Siberian
Plateau

Sea of
Okhotsk

40°N

EUROPE

ALPS

Mount Blanc

El'brus
18,510 ft
5,642 m
Black Sea

Volga R.

The Steppes

Caspian Sea
-92 ft
-28 m

Altay Mountains

Mongolian
Plateau

GOBI

NORTH

PACIFIC

OCEAN

A S I A

Tian Shah

K2

Plateau
of
Tibet

Mt. Everest
29,035 ft
8,850 m

Yellow R.

Mediterranean Sea

Syrian
Desert

Dead Sea
-1,399 ft
-408 m

HIMALAYA

Great
Indian
Desert

TROPIC OF CANCER

20°N

A R A

Nile R.

Red Sea

Arabian
Peninsula

Empty Quarter

Deccan
Plateau

Bay
of
Bengal

Indochina
Peninsula

Philippine
Sea

H E L

Tibesti

Arabian
Sea

South China Sea

M i c r o n e s i a

Guinea

Lake Assal
-512 ft
-156 m

Ethiopian
Highlands

Melanesia

AFRICA

Congo
Basin

Lake
Victoria

Kilimanjaro
19,336 ft
5,895 m

Sumatra

Borneo

Java

I n d o n e s i a

New
Guinea

EQUATOR

0°

Lower Guinea

Mitumba Mts.

Lake
Tanganyika

Lake
Malawi

INDIAN

Madagascar

AUSTRALIA

Coral
Sea

Kalahari
Desert

OCEAN

Western
Plateau

Lake Eyre
-52 ft
-16 m

TROPIC OF CAPRICORN

20°S

Thabana Ntlenyana

SOUTH

PACIFIC

OCEAN

Mt. Kosciuszko
7,310 ft
2,228 m

Tasman
Sea

Tasmania

New Zealand

40°S

60°S

ANTARCTIC CIRCLE

Queen Maud Land

Wilkes Land

80°S

20°E   40°E   60°E   80°E   100°E   120°E   140°E   160°E

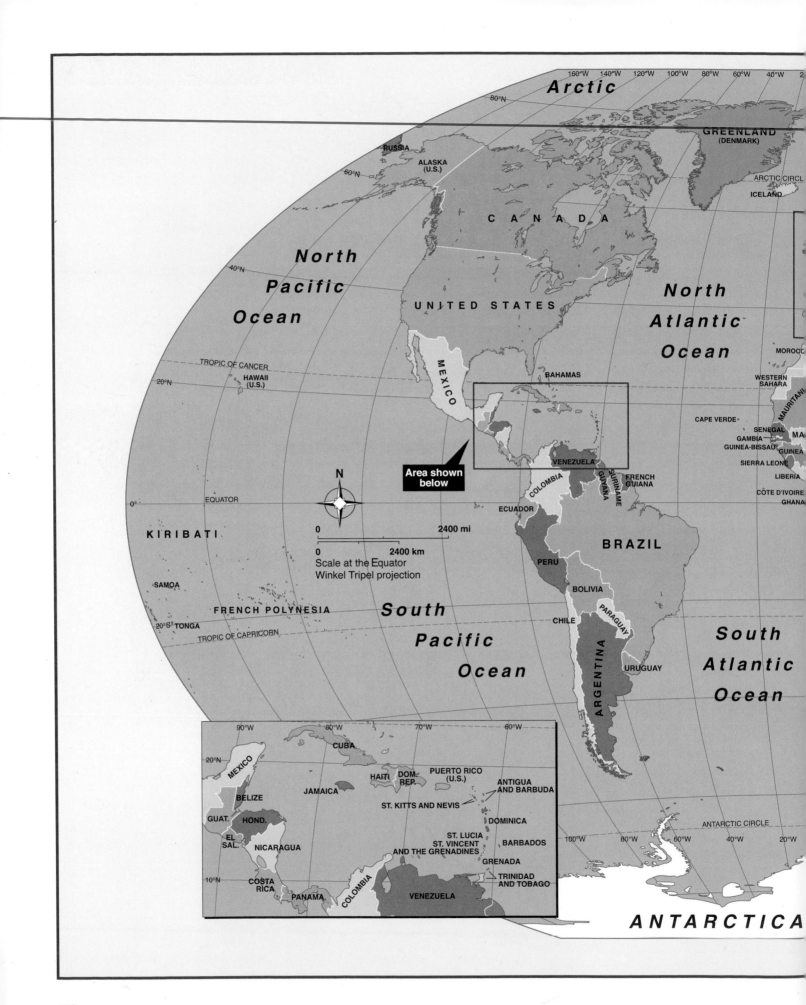

Arctic

160°W 140°W 120°W 100°W 80°W 60°W 40°W

80°N

GREENLAND
(DENMARK)

RUSSIA

ALASKA
(U.S.)

ARCTIC CIRCLE

60°N

ICELAND

C A N A D A

North
Pacific
Ocean

North
Atlantic
Ocean

40°N

UNITED STATES

MOROCC

TROPIC OF CANCER

BAHAMAS

WESTERN
SAHARA

20°N

HAWAII
(U.S.)

CAPE VERDE

SENEGAL
GAMBIA
GUINEA-BISSAU
SIERRA LEONE
LIBERIA
CÔTE D'IVOIRE
GHANA

MAURITANI

MA

GUINEA

VENEZUELA

SURINAME
GUYANA

FRENCH
GUIANA

COLOMBIA

Area shown
below

N

ECUADOR

0°

EQUATOR

KIRIBATI

0   2400 mi

PERU

BRAZIL

0   2400 km

Scale at the Equator
Winkel Tripel projection

BOLIVIA

SAMOA

PARAGUAY

FRENCH POLYNESIA

South
Pacific
Ocean

CHILE

South
Atlantic
Ocean

20°S TONGA

TROPIC OF CAPRICORN

ARGENTINA

URUGUAY

90°W   80°W   70°W   60°W

20°N

CUBA

ANTARCTIC CIRCLE

MEXICO

PUERTO RICO
(U.S.)

100°W   80°W   60°W   40°W   20°W

HAITI DOM.
REP.

ANTIGUA
AND BARBUDA

JAMAICA

BELIZE

ST. KITTS AND NEVIS

GUAT.

HOND.

DOMINICA

EL
SAL.

NICARAGUA

ST. LUCIA
ST. VINCENT
AND THE GRENADINES

BARBADOS

10°N

GRENADA

COSTA
RICA

TRINIDAD
AND TOBAGO

PANAMA

COLOMBIA

VENEZUELA

ANTARCTICA

70

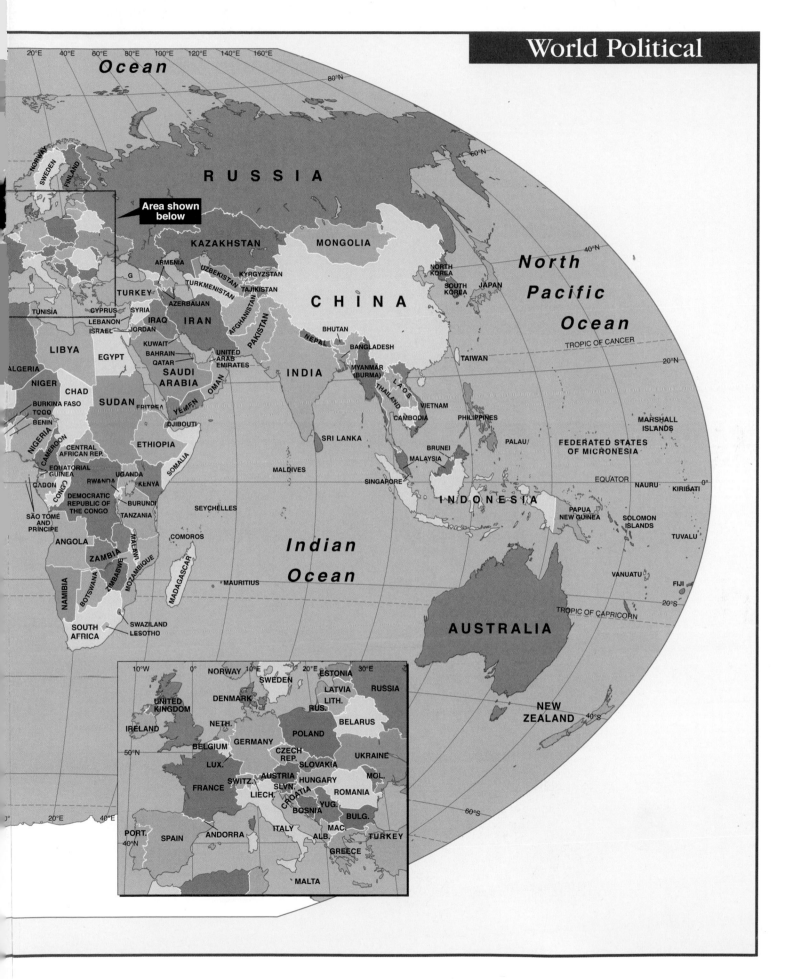

Ocean

20°E 40°E 60°E 80°E 100°E 120°E 140°E 160°E

80°N

RUSSIA

Area shown below

60°N

KAZAKHSTAN

MONGOLIA

40°N

North

Pacific

Ocean

ARMENIA
UZBEKISTAN KYRGYZSTAN
TURKMENISTAN TAJIKISTAN

NORTH KOREA
SOUTH KOREA JAPAN

TURKEY
AZERBAIJAN

CHINA

CYPRUS SYRIA
TUNISIA
LEBANON IRAQ IRAN
ISRAEL JORDAN
AFGHANISTAN
PAKISTAN

TAIWAN

TROPIC OF CANCER

BHUTAN
NEPAL
BANGLADESH

20°N

LIBYA
EGYPT
KUWAIT
BAHRAIN
QATAR
UNITED ARAB EMIRATES

SAUDI ARABIA

INDIA

MYANMAR (BURMA)
LAOS
THAILAND
VIETNAM

ALGERIA

NIGER
CHAD
SUDAN
OMAN
YEMEN
ERITREA
DJIBOUTI

CAMBODIA

PHILIPPINES

MARSHALL ISLANDS

BURKINA FASO
TOGO
BENIN
NIGERIA
CAMEROON
CENTRAL AFRICAN REP.
ETHIOPIA

SRI LANKA

BRUNEI
MALAYSIA

PALAU

FEDERATED STATES OF MICRONESIA

EQUATORIAL GUINEA
GABON
CONGO
RWANDA
UGANDA
KENYA
SOMALIA

MALDIVES

SINGAPORE

EQUATOR

NAURU

KIRIBATI
0°

DEMOCRATIC REPUBLIC OF THE CONGO
BURUNDI
TANZANIA

SEYCHELLES

INDONESIA

SÃO TOMÉ AND PRÍNCIPE

PAPUA NEW GUINEA

SOLOMON ISLANDS

ANGOLA
ZAMBIA
MALAWI
COMOROS

Indian

TUVALU

NAMIBIA
ZIMBABWE
MOZAMBIQUE
MADAGASCAR

Ocean

MAURITIUS

VANUATU

FIJI

BOTSWANA

20°S

TROPIC OF CAPRICORN

SOUTH AFRICA
SWAZILAND
LESOTHO

AUSTRALIA

NEW ZEALAND

40°S

60°S

Inset map (Europe):

10°W 0° NORWAY 10°E 20°E ESTONIA 30°E
SWEDEN LATVIA RUSSIA
UNITED KINGDOM DENMARK LITH.
RUS. BELARUS
IRELAND NETH.
BELGIUM GERMANY POLAND
LUX. CZECH REP. UKRAINE
SLOVAKIA
FRANCE SWITZ. AUSTRIA HUNGARY MOL.
LIECH. SLVN. ROMANIA
CROATIA
BOSNIA YUG. BULG.
PORT. ITALY MAC.
SPAIN ANDORRA ALB. TURKEY
GREECE
MALTA

50°N
40°N
20°E 40°E

Credits

Map Essentials: Student Book is produced through the worldwide resources of the National Geographic Society, John M. Fahey, Jr., *President and Chief Executive Officer;* Gilbert M. Grosvenor, *Chairman of the Board;* Nina D. Hoffman, *Senior Vice President, Publications.*

PREPARED BY NATIONAL GEOGRAPHIC SCHOOL PUBLISHING
Ericka Markman, *Vice President and Director;* Steve Mico, *Editorial Director;* Richard Easby, *Editorial Manager;* Lydia Lewis, *Editor;* Kate Hardcastle, *Associate Editor;* Jim Hiscott, *Design Manager;* Matt Wascavage, *Production Manager;* Rick Bounds, *Manufacturing.*

Production: Clifton M. Brown III, *Manufacturing and Quality Control.*

EDITORIAL DEVELOPMENT AND PRODUCTION MANAGEMENT
Summer Street Press
Judy Glickman and Nick Mandelkern, *Editorial Directors;* Laura DeLallo, *Editor;* Janet McHugh, *Writer;* Paula Jo Smith, *Production;* Dallas Chang, *Photography Research*

MAPS
Equator Graphics
National Geographic Maps (cover map)

PHOTOGRAPHS
(main image) ©M-SAT Corporation, *www.TheWorldFromSpace;* **(child with globe)** Kuchik Photography; **page 5** AP/World Wide; **Page 8** Tom Van Sant/Stock Market; **page 9** Victor Boswell/NGS Image Collection; **page 10** Keren Su/Stock Boston; **page 13** Chris Johns/NGS Image Collection; **page 14** Randy Ury/The Stock Market; **page 17** Laurence R. Lowry/Stock Boston; **page 19** Martin Rogers/Martin Rogers Photography; **page 20** US Air Force/FPG International; **page 23** George F. Mobley/NGS Image Collection; **page 25** Cary Wolinsky/NGS Image Collection; **page 26** Frank & Helen Schreider/NGS Image Collection; **page 31** Victor Boswell/NGS; **page 33** Laurant Van der Stockt/Liaison Agency; **page 35** Mark Peterson/SABA; **page 39** Bonnie Kamin/Index Stock; **page 41** Ken Straiton/The Stock Market; **page 42** Univ. of Miami/NGS Image Collection; **page 45** James P. Blair/NGS Image Collection; **page 46** Hulton Getty/Liaison Agency; **page 49** Najlah Feanny/SABA; **page 50** Robert Gale/Liaison Agency; **page 52** W. T. Sullivan III/Science Photo Library/Photo Researchers; **page 53** David Sailors/The Stock Market; **page 54** Scripps Institute of Oceanography/NGS Image Collection; **page 56** NASA/Liaison Agency; **page 58** National Geographic Society